ISBN 978-1-332-15119-6
PIBN 10291528

This book is a reproduction of an important historical work. Forgotten Books uses
state-of-the-art technology to digitally reconstruct the work, preserving the original format
whilst repairing imperfections present in the aged copy. In rare cases, an imperfection in
the original, such as a blemish or missing page, may be replicated in our edition. We do,
however, repair the vast majority of imperfections successfully; any imperfections that
remain are intentionally left to preserve the state of such historical works.

1 MONTH OF
FREE
READING
at
www.ForgottenBooks.com

By purchasing this book you are eligible for one month membership to ForgottenBooks.com, giving you unlimited access to our entire collection of over 700,000 titles via our web site and mobile apps.

To claim your free month visit:

www.forgottenbooks.com/free291528

FATHER BERNARD DONNELLY

The Life of Father Bernard Donnelly

WITH HISTORICAL SKETCHES

of

KANSAS CITY, ST. LOUIS

and

INDEPENDENCE, MISSOURI

By

Rev. William J. Dalton

Published by
GRIMES-JOYCE PRINTING COMPANY
Kansas City, Missouri
1921

GB

Imprimatur

✠ Thomas F. Lillis, D. D.
Bishop of Kansas City, Missouri

October 8th, 1921

To
KANSAS CITY

The home of Father Donnelly
The city of his heart
The scene of his great efforts
The result of his aspirations
The mighty metropolis he foretold

This biography is dedicated

CONTENTS

INTRODUCTION
BY THE AUTHOR

Bishop Louis Wm. V. Dubourg of New Orleans, but living in St. Louis, wrote on January 30th, 1826, to his brother· "I have long been convinced that nothing could be accomplished here without the religious orders. A man living isolated from his kind grows weary of the apparent uselessness of his efforts. The intense heat exhausts his strength and checks his ardor. Too often he loses his life or in the fear of losing it he abandons his post. He is fortunate indeed if he does not prove the truth of those words of the Holy Ghost: 'Woe to him who is alone!' and from a being full of vigor and activity he becomes a good-for-nothing and the scorn of his fellowmen." (St. Louis Catholic Historical Review, Vol. II, Nos. 2-3, p. 70.)

The Right Reverend Bishop was not living alone; he had vicars-general and priests living around him, and surely had no reason to get weary, but he accepted a promotion, becoming ar archbishop in France.

How the hundreds of missionaries "living isolated," like Fathers Badin and Nerinckx, the founders of the Sisters of Charity and of Loretto in Kentucky, like Gallitzin, the Russian prince, in Pennsylvania, like Palamorgues in Iowa, Ravoux in the wilds of the Indian lands in Minnesota, like St. Cyr in Missouri and Illinois, and hundreds of other early missionaries from New Orleans to St. Louis, and westward to Oregon—Bishop Scanlon, the first pastor and bishop of Salt Lake, the bishops and priests of Idaho and Washington—how all those, "leading isolated lives," by their good work until death, successfully contradict the "conviction" of Bishop Dubourg! Fear of losing their lives did not make them abandon their posts. The glitter of archiepiscopal mitres could not win them back to easy lives in their own native lands.

Not every disposition is suited for a life of solitude, any more than every disposition is suited for a life in a community. Fathers Donnelly, Hammil and Fox of the St. Louis diocese, the diocesan pioneer priests in Illinois and along the Mississippi, Fathers John Bergier, Anthony Dayion, Michael Gaulin, Nicholas Foucault, John Daniel Tetu, and Francis Frison de Lamotte, are instances where the solitary life did not cool the missionary ardor.

The missionary who has a rugged constitution, whose soul is in his work, whose mind, like his health, is impervious to difficulties of climate and slow to give way under the strain of his efforts, and who, like St. Paul, sees only the greatness of the cause in which he is enrolled, does not crave or need the solace or support of companionship. Sympathy, cheering fellowship, constant advice and frequent suggestion would have hampered and discouraged the great Apostle of the Gentiles. We have reason to believe he could not have lived under the same roof with St. Peter. Shipwreck, now and then imprisonment in jails, opposition of false brethren, adversities of every kind, did not make him a good-for-nothing, isolated though he was.

There was a time not long ago when to touch upon the relative results of church activities among the missionary pioneers in America was to stir up a feeling bordering on rancor among the admirers of the various modern apostles. Admiring humanity will always divide on the question, who has done best? The early Christians were not exceptions. Some were for Paul, some for Apollo. St. Paul, in his first epistle to the Corinthians, writes:

"For while one saith: I indeed am of Paul; and another: I am of Apollo; are you not men? What then is Apollo and what is Paul? The min

isters of Him whom you have believed: and to
every one as the Lord hath given. I have planted,
Apollo watered: but God gave the increase."
(I Corinthians, lII: 4, 5, 6.)

All were loyal followers of the Twelve Apostles, and all full of praise of what each one did
in the advancement of Christianity. In science, in
art, in every phase of human excellence, men have
ever discussed the question, who is best, who leads
all the others? Tastes will differ. In the cause
of Christianity, the great chieftains present themselves in different lights to different people. Heroism has as many aspects as there are different
tastes and different ideas of what constitutes the
heroic. The twelve fearless Apostles appeal to
some, the martyrs to others, the sweet angelic
nature to others still. The spirit of organization,
banding an army by discipline and rules of forget-
fulness of self, awes many into an admiration of
system, and makes them forget or underestimate
the work of the units striving to the same end.
The universities of learning house great minds
struggling to forward every line of mental re-
search, yet the workshop here and there pro-
duces an Edison, who, singlehanded, brings out
results unsurpassed. When Oxford was at its
best, the literature of England was furnished by
the Addisons, the Goldsmiths, the Johnsons, in
the periodicals, and sometimes writing from the
very hovels of London. Yet the University in its
professors prospered and did much to enhance the
beauties and style of the English tongue.

In the missionary work of the world discovered by Columbus, the religious orders were first
in the field. From Quebec in Canada they tracked
the Indian tribes over plains and hills, along the
Atlantic coast. They looked them up first when
with Columbus they entered America. They

sought and found them on the banks of the St. Laurence, of the Great Lakes, of the Mississippi. About one hundred and fifty years afterwards they came to them and lived with them along the Missouri River, through the Great American Desert, over the Rocky Mountains, and, under De Smet, up into Oregon. The Jesuits, the Franciscans, the Benedictines, went into South America and preached Christ everywhere in that great division of the New World.

In this survey, where do we find the diocesan priests? In those days diocesan priests were in Europe in their respective territories, called dioceses. As their name indicates, they work within certain territorial lines. Their duty holds them to the people and the district to which they are assigned. They pledge themselves to labor at the call of their respective bishops. Besides, the diocesan priests were not numerous and there was not much scope for them. The religious orders were everywhere in Europe, monks and religious were numerous in cities, towns, and country places, too. The diocesan priest could not, if disposed, go into missionary fields. His salary kept him poor, in fact men rarely become rich from salary as a revenue. The diocesan priest is the bishop's priest and subject, and can go only where his bishop orders him. To enter the missionary career entailed the expense of travel from home across the Atlantic and to the scene of one's endeavors. The diocesan priest had very little, if any, money, not enough at least to pay his way to foreign lands. Had he the means to reach his destination he was without side money with which to feed and clothe himself. Even a religious order in financial straits would not look like a born missionary band in a new country.

Father Felix De Andreis was holy enough to be entered in the Process of Canonization, yet he was worldly wise. On February 24th, 1818, he wrote from St. Louis, where he had recently arrived, to his superior in Italy, Father Sicardi: "We need whole colonies of missionaries with considerable pecuniary resources, in order to make rapid progress in these intense woods." Father De Andreis knew the reputation of pioneer Christians and native Indians. The former had nothing to give the missionary, and the latter expected the missionary to give him help, for body as well as for soul. It costs a civilized man money to live even in the land of indolent savages, and though a man be a tailor and a cook he must pay for what he eats and wears even though he does put them together. Bishop Dubourg, who could turn a Latin sentence with Ciceronian ease and finesse and like a famed, gifted Irishman could say two things at the same time, minimized the value of the diocesan missionary because of the solitariness of his life and the lack of cheering surroundings, and preferred the religious communities to the one-man worker in the new countries. Another reason he had perhaps away down in his heart was that the monk or religious would not be dependent on the slim revenues of the Louisiana diocese. The Right Reverend Bishop was a man of zeal and brave heart, but he remained a rather long time in Paris because he wanted to secure the means to live in a manner becoming his dignity when he should go to his western diocese. He could not husband the means he was securing in Paris if he were obliged to support or even aid a band of diocesan priests. Bishop Dubourg knew that the diocesan priest would be next to useless without some help to keep him in the wilds of the new West. So also would the religious orders. It

would have added to the straightforwardness of
his character had he said with the sainted Father
De Andreis: "We need, we can use, whole colonies of those priests only 'who have considerable
pecuniary resources, to work and make progress
in these intense forests.'"

European nations with foreign possessions in
Asia, Africa, or the islands, always find a ready,
necessary and efficient helper in the Christian missionary. Their claims over their possessions are
strengthened and made easy by the mollifying, re-
straining efforts of the ministers of God. Their
soldiers need and demand the ministrations of the
chaplains. Even France, when she was closing the
churches at home and driving the religious orders
out of the Republic, would send to the colonies an
army to punish insults to the French missionaries or
refusals to receive them. Infidelity might be the
proper thing at home, but the conquered pagan in
the French possessions needed religion, and France
at least forced them to listen to the missisionaries
and not dare molest them. Perhaps they sought not
so much the religious impressions and conversions
made by the missionaries as the obedience to government authority taught by the Church. And having
sent missionaries to their foreign acquisitions, does
it not seem reasonable to say they supported them,
as England sustained the Catholic priests in the
West Indies.

The Jesuits in the Canadian territory along the
lakes had blazed the way for a new race of missionaries. They had explored the new country, and
made known the topography and even the very nature of the soil of every place they visited. Their
first work was done, and another awaited them.
They were skilled scientists, and were by training
at home professors and founders of schools and colleges. Others could follow in their footsteps over

mountain and vale, for the Jesuits furnished the world with maps of the pathways and streams of Canada and the northeast States. Then they returned to fulfill the second part of their oath-bound obligation, "to take special care of the education of youth."

Father Charles Van Quickenborne, superior of the small colony of two Jesuit Fathers, seven aspirants to the priesthood, and three lay brothers, had been in Missouri but a very short time when he undertook his first missionary tour among the Osage Indians in the Territory in 1827. His first visit to the Indians convinced him that no great or permanent results could ever be accomplished among the indolent, wandering and indocile aborigines of the woods and prairies, "which would at all compensate missionaries for sacrificing all their energies and resources in exclusive attention to the savages." (See Father Walter Hill's "History of St. Louis University.") Strong language? Well, St. Paul used strong language about the people to whom he preached. An easy, generous critic might say Father Van Quickenborne's language was that of a chiding mother to her indifferent boy. Whatever way it may sound, it was a warning that the Jesuits had other aims in their good work than sacrificing their resources and available properties in futile missions among the Indians. Bishop Rosatti about that time was anxious to rid himself of a high school or college belonging to the diocese of St. Louis. The Jesuits soon became owners of it and gave most of their time and labor to the college. And what a blessing to religion in St. Louis and the United States at large that college has been under the masterful leadership of the Jesuits for nearly one hundred years! Father Van Quickenborne and Father Hoecken, the two Fathers Eysvogels, were living with the Indians in the Territory in 1836 and 1837, and in fact through their successors at St. Mary's, Kansas, are with them yet—that is, if there are any Indians left there.

Rome saw that the religious communities were tiring and seeking other fields, so the Propaganda requested that missionary colleges be started in Ireland, France, Belgium and Spain. The bishops of America, with new dioceses in the north and west, found in the priest-graduates of these colleges men willing and able to carry on the unfinished work of the first missionaries. No greater zeal, no more heroic endurance of bitter hardships, ever marked the lives of apostles in God's service than were displayed by Father (afterwards Bishop) Baraga and his successors for years in the cold north peninsula of Michigan. Bishop M. Loras of Dubuque and Bishop Joseph Cretin of St. Paul were aided to wonderful mission results among Indians and pioneers. They were all diocesan priests trained for the requirements of those early days. Bishop Martin Henni, the first Bishop of Milwaukee, gradually found vocations at home among the diocesan students of his seminary.

Nearly one hundred years ago the Lazarists in St. Louis prepared diocesan students for missionary labors in Missouri, Kansas and Louisiana. The priests of the diocese were soon as efficient in this western wilderness as the Fathers of religious orders had been in primitive times. They, too, soon became as inured to the dangers to life and limb as were their predecessors. And how many and how severe were their endurances! They frequently lived in huts without cooks and without help, and without nurses in sickness and accidents. The religious had all their struggles with rain and swollen streams, with miasmatic poisons in new and savage countries, but they had the fraternal care of their own brothers who nursed them and they had their mother-house for a hospital when that was necessary. The religious missioners had to strive for means of livelihood, but in crying need they had the financial resources of their order to draw upon. In 1840 Fathers Verreydt and De Smet, the one on his way to St. Mary's Mission, the other on his way to the Oregon missions, met at Kanzas, now Kansas City. They both were in pressing want for articles of food and wear. They made purchases at the Chouteau warehouse. In payment they presented drafts on Father Verhaegen, then Vice-Provincial at St. Louis University. The drafts were honored as cash. Imagine a Donnelly or a St. Cyr drawing on their worthy Bishop at St. Louis! Their draft might be honored by the drawee, but a repetition would be unthought of, because of the warning letter which certainly would have followed. The diocesan missionary was like the Indian small boy whose father would pitch him into the fast current—it was a case of sink or swim.

However, there were zealous men willing and unafraid, who, without financial support from religious order or other source, undertook the missionary life in localities where they could hope for only the most meager if any returns in a worldly sense, men who faced hardships of all kinds in a life new to their own experience, who overcame obstacles of a sort to discourage the bravest, and who, strong in Faith and purpose, toiled on in God's holy service until able to do no more, and who with their parting sigh could whisper a happy "Deo gratias," content in the knowledge that their efforts had not been unavailing, that what they had so painfully struggled for had been gained, and that it was all for God's greater glory. Not least among such valiant ones was Father Bernard Donnelly, the story of whose life is recorded in these pages.

At an age when youthful ardor had cooled, with a true idea of what confronted him, with the knowledge of mission life in the far West imprinted on his mind from books and from the lips of the early missionaries in Missouri and the Territory, Father Donnelly faced his chosen career undaunted. Through malarial chill and fever, time and time again, through the bitter cold of winter and the burning heat of summer, through trackless desert and over untrod hills and mountains, among kind but poor and thriftless squatters and unsuccessful people of western Missouri and Arkansas, with a cheerless, fireless hut to enter when long tours were over, without cook, without nurse or doctor, he struggled on. The strong frame weakened, the limbs lost their agility and the joints their suppleness, the lungs resented the cold air of the prairie and the mountain, and a cough preceded the wheezing short breath of the victim of asthma, his fingers were misshapen from many a rheumatic attack and from exposure in blizzards, but he never yielded to discouragement; with a smile on his face and cheer in his heart to the very end he said his daily Mass, was ready to answer calls to the sick and the dying, and was ever attentive to all the demands of duty.

CHAPTER I.

EARLY LIFE.

BERNARD DONNELLY was born in the town of Kilnacreva, County Cavan, Ireland. The day and year of his birth, had he ever known, he forgot in his advanced years. He knew he was baptized in infancy, for the priest who performed the ceremony was his pastor up to manhood and often told him so. The rule of the Catholic Church is that the priest must make the record of each baptism, giving the date of the baptism, the name of the child, the date of its birth, the names of the parents and the names of the sponsors, together with his own name as the priest who baptized the child.

When young Donnelly was born and for years before and afterwards, the English laws forbade a Catholic priest to make any record or keep any entry of a baptism. Schools were not tolerated in Ireland when Bernard's parents were young. The school teacher in Ireland was outlawed by the English government, a price was put on his head and he was hunted like a wild beast. So his father and mother were unable to read or write, and records of their children's birth could not be made by them. When asked his age he would make a calculation by saying he could recall such and such an historic event and so must have been five or six years old at that time. From his recollection of events recorded on the tablets of his memory and connected with the career of Napoleon Bonaparte, he would say: "Well, I am older than the 19th Century." The small boy early picks out his hero, who must be a fighter on the field of battle or in the arena, and he never forgets his name or deeds.

His father's name was John Donnelly and his mother's was Rose Fox. A little while before Bernard reached school age, the English rulers of Ireland had discovered that keeping Ireland in enforced illiteracy did not make the Irish more docile subjects nor did it turn them into cringing slaves. This kind of persecution drove the young manhood of Ireland by the thousands into the army of France. The famed victory of Fontenoy, May 11th, 1745, when the English army was almost destroyed, sent the echo of the cheers of the Irish troops under Marshal Saxe across the ocean from Belgium into every town and city of England. And those exultant cheers of revenge rolled around the halls of the English parliament and made terror-stricken legislators repeal one brutal law after another. Schools were among the last of all concessions granted Ireland, but those schools were opened and maintained by the Irish themselves.

The days of the hedge school were past: when the teacher, disguised, hid himself in the forest or mountain crags, where his pupils flocked to learn the rudiments of knowledge as well as the languages of Greek and Latin, and higher mathematics. The new schools were poor in construction and poor in furnishment. To a makeshift like this young Donnelly trudged along, happy and ambitious to learn. Six days a week he carried his slate and "cutter," his quill pen and drying sand for his freshly written page, to the teacher's home where school was held. A block of turf was the pupil's daily contribution towards heating the room, and once a week each scholar handed the teacher as many pennies as he could afford for tuition.

There were no readers for the standards as we have, and after learning the alphabet and mastering the spelling of words of one syllable, the pupils had to reach words of two syllables through books of ad-

venture, of history, and of religious devotion. Such
a faulty arrangement made the reading of simple
words a work of years. Practical men all over Ireland soon saw the lack of system in the new schools.
Committees were formed from all parts of Ireland
to advance and simplify the method of imparting
knowledge. Children were classified, more methodical men succeeded the early schoolmaster, and
suitable and comfortable buildings were erected
everywhere.

Young Donnelly was a pupil in time to benefit
by the change for the better. His talent and application soon entitled him to promotion to a higher
grade of studies, and his parents placed him under
the care of one of the many teachers who specialized
in mathematics. His name was Hugh O'Reilly. He
lived at Cooteshill, a short distance from Donnelly's
home. O'Reilly's reputation was known far and
wide. Under him the youth acquired a knowledge of
algebra, geometry and trigonometry. His next
ambition was a course of English and civil engineering. For these he put himself under the tuition of
a George Alderson, a graduate of Oxford and for
years a professor of engineering in a military
academy near Oxford. Alderson's school at this time
was in the outskirts of Dublin. In his second year
here Donnelly resumed his studies of Latin and
Greek. After three years of hard study Dr. Alderson pronounced Donnelly worthy the highest honors
of his class. His school days in Ireland were now
over. Recommendation from Alderson secured for
his pupil a membership in a civil engineering corps
in Dublin. His next location was in Liverpool, where
he worked as civil engineer in the construction of
the Liverpool docks.

A good salary and a saving disposition enabled
him to help his parents in Ireland and to put away
some money every month to pay his passage to

America in the near future. Like thousands of his countrymen young and old he saw the goal of future success across the ocean. His parents were then, and while he was at school, the objects of his solicitude. He found time while studying in Ireland to put aside his books now and then to return to his home to help his father on the little farm rented from a landlord. In evenings when the day's duties were done, he worked in stores and helped merchants in balancing their books. Even on holidays he found employment that brought tidy returns. He was ever a tireless student and a dutiful son.

In Liverpool he identified himself with various Catholic societies and sodalities, attending early Mass on his way to work every morning and approaching Holy Communion on Sundays. His exemplary life and scholarly attainments soon attracted the attention of the few priests then in Liverpool. They were his guides and his advisers, and by their influence put him in the way of the best Catholic society and found for him a home where he enjoyed every comfort. Father Theobald Matthew's crusade against intemperance was fast winning the blessings of the world. He had torn thousands of helpless victims from the clutches of the monster drunkenness. Overindulgence in strong liquor had swept over England, Scotland and Ireland. Liverpool was a workingman's city. Drunkenness often works its worst ravages among the people of toil and few comforts. Bernard Donnelly soon perceived the fell effects of liquor in the ranks of the toilers on the wharves and in the workshops. He saw many of his own countrymen, who came to Liverpool to get employment to help themselves and their poor families in Ireland, become slaves to the whisky habit. In young manhood as in after life when a priest he had a heart and a ready will for the unfortunate.

After consulting his priest friends he started a temperance society. They were with him and encouraged and blessed his undertaking. The Catholic pulpits announced the time and place of the meetings. A large hall could not hold the crowds that responded. Every priest in Liverpool and priests from surrounding towns were on the platform. Their presence was a benediction and their speeches were eloquent in approval and strong in appeal to join the cause.

Bernard Donnelly's name was a signal for loud applause. With an outburst of unanimity he was appointed chairman. The Mayor of Liverpool thanked the young chairman for such a society and one so much needed. Although not a Catholic, he requested that his name be enrolled. Before the meeting adjourned Donnelly was elected president. More than seven hundred men and women responded to Mr. Donnelly's appeals by then and there joining Father Matthew's Temperance Society of the City of Liverpool. The large audience arose and with right hands uplifted repeated the temperance pledge authorized by Father Matthew. The Vicar General read the pledge from a letter of approval and blessing written by Father Matthew at his headquarters in Cork, Ireland.

For some weeks Mr. Donnelly attended meetings held in various parts of the city of Liverpool. The meetings grew in attendance and the membership enrolled kept pace, until Mr. Donnelly was able to announce the new crusade eight thousand strong. It was not long until Father Matthew tore himself away from his great work at home and followed in the wake of the young local organizer. He opened every meeting with words of praise and thanks to Mr. Donnelly, whom he named the "Apostle of Temperance in England." Father Matthew went back to Ireland but in a little while returned to England

and lectured in every large city, praising everywhere
the work of his young countryman.

In 1849-1852 Father Matthew visited the United
States. He lectured on his heart subject in every
Catholic church and many halls from Boston to New
Orleans and St. Louis. In the city of Washington
he was honored by an invitation from both houses
of Congress to address them in the Senate Chamber. While lecturing in St. Louis in October, 1850,
the pastor of Independence, Missouri, called on him
in the residence of Archbishop Kenrick. The Bernard Donnelly who years previously had unfurled
the banner of Father Matthew in the city of Liverpool had become the priest Donnelly of Independence.
Words would fail to express the joyous hearts of
the great leader and the able lieutenant. When
they met in the Land of Promise and Freedom the
rugged frame of Father Matthew had been touched
by age and its infirmities, but his heart was as
benevolent and his voice as powerful and his work
as far-reaching as when last they were together.
America was as ready to recognize a benefactor of
the race as was England or Ireland. Father
Matthew was an orator and an orator is one who
persuades and captures. The American Senate and
House of Representatives pronounced him one of the
greatest orators that ever addressed their assembly.
America proclaimed him an orator by joining his
crusade in numbers over 500,000 strong.

A success in a most benevolent enterprise, with
a salary for his work as civil engineer and a surplus
with which to make the declining years of his
parents comfortable, and with fine prospects for
social and financial advance, Mr. Donnelly had
reasoned that his labors in Europe were complete.
He had a yearning for other surroundings. There
was an air of antiquity all about him from which he
wished to escape. His native land was crushed by

hundreds of years of oppression and ferocious cruelty. The very country he was leaving was the home of his country's oppressor. The very air he breathed was heavy with odors of prisons and jails. He felt enfettered, and he would be free. There is no freedom in a land where one's country and one's religion are hated.

Washington and his land of true democracy were his ideals of the hero to worship and the country to live in. Thousands of his fellow countrymen were happy across the Atlantic and many of them were writing him to join them. He had a secret deep down in his heart which he seldom, if ever, divulged. He believed he was called to be a priest. He would be received readily into the sacred ministry in England or in his dear old Ireland. He was more than once told so by clergymen high in the ranks of the priesthood. But he would rather be what he often called a free priest, secure from unfriendly national laws and interferences of an inimical government. With that truly Irish and comical twinkle of eye he often said, "I believe there are other ways of going to Heaven than through martyrdom." He made up his mind to go to America and there serve in the priesthood. Ireland had enough of priests, America needed more. He bade farewell to Liverpool and his many friends there and returned to Ireland. He spent some months with his parents and then took shipping for New York. Fulton's steamboats were still on trial. Steam propelled the light craft along the banks of the Hudson River and frightened the Indians and the western pioneers on the Mississippi and the Missouri, but had not yet proved secure to the timid passengers crossing the broad and turbulent Atlantic Ocean. The sailing vessel that he selected was packed with his countrypeople, like himself fleeing from misery. The passage was anything but pleasant. There were few comforts on board, many were sick from the roughness of the sea. The time crossing was eighty days.

One of the first men he became acquainted with on landing in New York, and that was through letters of introduction, was a Mr. O'Connor, a school teacher in New York, the father of Charles O'Connor, America's greatest constitutional lawyer. It was a pleasing surprise to find that many of his countrymen were school teachers in the cities of America from New York to the farthest western city, St. Louis, in Philadelphia, Charleston and New Orleans. They were in nearly every city on the Ohio River, and in Cincinnati. Everywhere the Irish schoolmaster wielded the rod and taught the young idea how to shoot.

Daniel Boone accepted an invitation to colonize the territory of Missouri. He entered many acres of land at Point de Femme, about the site of St. Charles. He brought with him Marylanders, Carolinians, Kentuckians, Tennesseeans, and two Irish school teachers to instruct the children in the rudiments of learning. Neither Boone nor his followers had the advantage of education. Boone's school teachers were versed in many things. They could out jump, out wrestle, out box, and out run the nimblest of the semi-wild men they accompanied. In the school the teacher's rod was as essential as the book or the slate, pen or paper. The rod was as necessary to the teacher in his realm as the royal sceptre to the King of England on the opening of Parliament. It was a sign to the pupil that the law of order was presiding. In the Irish teacher's hand the ruler was a connecting link between teacher and pupil, with the pupil at the end that brought shock and pain. He used the ruler, as he was wont to say, to drive learning into the pupil when the easier or more gentle method failed.

CHAPTER II.

MR. DONNELLY BECOMES A SCHOOL TEACHER.

MR. DONNELLY while in Ireland had practiced the profession of school teacher. At short intervals he supplied the places of two different teachers while studying in the city of Dublin. He also filled a vacancy in a school in his native county where in youth he had been a pupil. His friends in New York suggested that he take a school in either New York or Philadelphia. Philadelphia was a close rival of New York in those days and the salaries offered by directors of education were higher in Philadelphia. Besides, Mr. Donnelly had the county clannishness then and in fact all through life: he leaned to men from his own county in Ireland. Philadelphia then and for many years after was the stopping place in America for men from Donegal and Cavan. They flocked there. He selected Philadelphia where he could hear the soft brogue of the North of Ireland and where he could enjoy the fellowship of his own townsland people. He accepted the offer of a well equipped school and a very desirable salary. After a year and more he was offered a better school in Pittsburgh with increased remuneration.

Clerical friends among the Dominican Fathers in Ohio, old friends and companions in Ireland, induced him to come close to them in Lancaster, Ohio. This invitation westward was backed by a letter from the Hon. Thomas Ewing, Senator from Ohio from 1831 to 1837, and afterwards Secretary of the Interior, and father-in-law of General Sherman. He was Secretary of the Treasury under President Harrison in 1841, Secretary of the Interior under President Taylor in 1849, and then Justice of the Supreme Court.

Lancaster at that time was the residence town of some of the oldest and wealthiest families of Ohio. The West was no longer an unknown land to the Atlantic front of our country. Cincinnati was recognized as the point where civilization was free from the presence of the red-man. The few railroads skirted along the Atlantic coast and were more or less an experiment. Capital could not think of risking tunnels through the mountains or of building over them for a few scattered citizens living along western water streams. Flatboats were creaking under the weight of freight from Pittsburgh to Cincinnati and west to where the Ohio mingles with the Mississippi. Passenger steamboats were sources of pleasure and convenience for the west and southbound passengers on the Ohio. Cincinnati was to the Ohio River what New York, Boston and Philadelphia were to the Atlantic Ocean —it was a point of entry and exit. The Cincinnatian was growing in wealth and he needed a suburban town in which to sleep, to live, and to have his children educated, and Lancaster shared this benefit with Somerset. Mr. Donnelly grasped this offer to teach the "gentry's" children. It is not a weakness in nature to look high and go upwards. Donnelly was quick in taking advantage of such an opportunity. Upon his arrival in Lancaster he was welcomed by Father Martin and Father Young, Dominican priests. They introduced him to Senator Ewing. Mrs. Ewing was a Catholic and insisted that the new teacher should consider her house his home. Some of the Ewing children were among the first enrolled in his school. While in Lancaster, Mr. Donnelly was treated as one of the Ewing household. In after years when Mr. Donnelly was the Catholic pastor of Kansas City, Hugh Boyle Ewing,

the son of Senator Ewing, and William Tecumseh
Sherman, the son-in-law of Senator Ewing, were
practicing law at Leavenworth, Kansas (1858-9).
They renewed their old acquaintance and visited
each other frequently.

Father Donnelly until his last sickness kept
"The School Roll" of his pupils at Lancaster. But
the pupil he was proudest of and whose deeds of
valor and generalship he was forever extolling was
General Philip Henry Sheridan. The General's
father was born in County Cavan and that fact was
something Father Donnelly never failed to mention
in his reminiscent moods. The General wrote his
memoirs a few years before his death. He gave
some space in the book to schoolboy days. He tells
some interesting and amusing stories of his Irish
schoolmaster in Ohio. While paying tribute to the
ability of the teacher, he lauds his cunning. He tells
that whenever anything serious went amiss he never
failed punishing the guilty youth, for he always
flogged the whole school. But for the teacher, Mr.
Donnelly, then a priest, he substituted another name.
When General Sheridan was in charge of the middle
or western division of the army, with headquarters
in Chicago, he frequently stopped over at Kansas
City on his way west or from Kansas during the
Indian uprisings. He invariably called on Father
Donnelly. The General was a good raconteur and
told many amusing stories of the days under Father
Donnelly's tutorship. He would say to Father Donnelly: "You were the best teacher I had before going to West Point—you were the only one." Father
Donnelly's repartee was: "Phil, you were my best
pupil. You rarely prepared your lessons, until after
a shaking up, and you trampled on every rule of the
school. But I always had a soft place in my heart
for you—you could whip every lad in the class."
When Sheridan, in 1879, was about to marry, he

wrote Father Donnelly inviting him to perform the
ceremony.   The old priest keenly appreciated the
honor, but sickness had weakened him and his end
was fast approaching, and he,could not comply.

While in Ohio Mr. Donnelly had a friend and
admirer in Archbishop Purcell of Cincinnati.   He
consulted the Archbishop on his vocation to the
priesthood.   Ohio seemed far west, but Donnelly expressed a preference for location and work farther
from the confines of civilization.   Ohio was well
dotted with growing towns.   He would prefer the
prairies or the mountains for health and labor, where
the laborers in the vineyard were few and far between.   Archbishop Purcell replied that he was sure
he would make an efficient priest and used his good
offices with Bishop Kenrick of St. Louis, to accept
his friend into the St. Louis diocese.   Mr. Donnelly
was immediately enrolled on the list of ecclesiastical
students for St. Louis and in a little while entered
St. Mary's Seminary of the Barrens, in Perry County, Missouri, eighty miles south of St. Louis.

Nicknaming has always been a strong habit in
America.   The "funny man" or the man who sees a
strong resemblance in a person or place to some condition or extravagance elsewhere, immediately rec-
ollects the likeness and to arouse a laugh mentions
what he imagines the original.   The aptness pro-
duces the laugh and a name is made which is last-
ing.   Perry County was covered with timber, but a
few spots of prairie were found here and there in
the woods.   These spots, barren of trees but rich in
productive soil, received among the pioneer settlers
the name of "barrens."   The name of a few spots
became the name of the surrounding country.   Here
in the spring of 1818 Bishop Dubourg located the
newly arrived Vincentian or Lazarist Fathers.   The
Superior of the Lazarists, Father Felix De Andreis,
who was born December 13th, 1778, at Demonte, a

considerable hamlet in the present diocese and former province of Cuneo, Piedmont, Italy, with four
priests and one lay brother, came from the city
of Rome at the invitation of Bishop Dubourg
and took charge of a college in St. Louis and
did missionary work among the pioneer Catholics in the vicinity.   Father De Andreis had
been a professor of theology in Rome from 1806
to 1815.   His learning and eloquence immediately
attracted the attention of the Eternal City.   Professors from the other colleges were often seen among
his auditors.   Cardinal Della Somaglia was a frequent listener to the young professor's lectures.   He
admired not only the solidity and beauty of his dis-
courses but the piety and unction with which he
spoke.   The Cardinal, in an audience with Pope Pius
VII, said: "Holy Father, I have found out lately a
treasure of science and piety in a priest of the Mission at Monte Citorio; his name is Felix De Andreis
and he is yet quite young.   I heard him speak several times on the dignity and duties of the priesthood and he pleased me much, so that I seemed to
hear a St. John Chrysostom or a St. Bernard."   En-
raptured at these words, the Sovereign Pontiff
immediately replied: "We must not lose sight of
this young man, for it is with such as he that we
should fill the episcopal sees."
    In one of the most perilous and prolonged
pontificates in the history of the Church, his king-
dom wrested from him, his city robbed of most
precious inheritances, the sanctuaries despoiled of
costly gifts, his libraries and art galleries laid bare
of their books and paintings, and he himself a
prisoner in another land, with war raging the
world over, millions of his children murdered to
satisfy the ambition of a man who laughed at him
and defied him, Pius VII lost sight of the young
man so worthy of the episcopate.   And how for-

tunate for the young man that fate did not give
him the mitre! He would have died in some ob-
scure diocese with a world of good never accomplished. Instead, he breathed his last after years
spent in the great work of helping mankind spiritually and mentally. He leaves the impress of
his plans and the wishes of his soul on the great
men who followed where he began. His sanctity
and learning were perpetuated in the Rosatti, the
De Neckere, the Odin, the Timon, the Ryan, the
Lynch, the Amat, archbishops and bishops, all
learned and holy men. He lives in the lives of
the hundreds of able professors and true exem-
plars of piety and learning who taught and teach
in the seminaries and colleges and universities at
the Barrens, Cape Girardeau, New Orleans, Niag-
ara Falls, Brooklyn, Germantown, Chicago, Dal-
las, Denver, Los Angeles, and the Kenrick Seminary of St. Louis. The eminent Professor Torna-
tori, to whose training in learning and sanctity
the American Church is indebted for its greatest
light in the Episcopacy, Francis Patrick Kenrick,
Archbishop of Baltimore, was a Lazarist professor
at Rome and at the Barrens. Fathers Alizeri and
Lavazeri, Lazarists both, gave a fame to their
Father De Andreis by their lore and the training
imparted to the priests and bishops who studied
under them. The Very Reverend Father John
McGary, the second superior of Mount St. Mary's,
Emmetsburg, who saw a genius in the young John
Hughes, the gardener, and trained him for the
priesthood and lived to see him the immortal Archbishop of New York, left his Eastern home and
joined the Lazarists and spent the last thirty years
of his long life as a professor at Cape Girardeau.

CHAPTER III.

HE BECOMES A PRIEST.

IT was to the Barrens Mr. Donnelly traced his steps when he left his school at Lancaster to prepare for tne priesthood. His knowledge of higher mathematics, of English, Greek and Latin, brought him up to philosophy and theology, and gave him time to aid the professors in the branches in which he ably qualified. He never tired of telling of the happy days he spent at the Barrens. He mentioned the names of every professor during and before his time, and could tell where and when they were born and the date of each one's death. Gratitude was a part of his nature: he never forgot a kindness, and, to be true to the real man, he never forgot any act of unkindness done him.

Nearly three years of study and preparation for the priesthood brought him up to the Sanctuary. He was ordained priest by Bishop P. R. Kenrick in the year 1845.

Father Patrick O'Brien, who built St. John's and St. Michael's churches in St. Louis, a man of great piety and well grounded in theology and a student all his life, always referred to his old classmate, Bernard Donnelly, as the brightest scholar in his day at the Barrens. Father William Wheeler, who for twenty-five years was a priest of St. Louis always connected with a city parish, was a graduate of Maynooth College, Ireland. He was ordained one year before Father Donnelly. After ordination he was appointed assistant to Father George Hamilton, who started St. Patrick's Parish but left for Boston before the completion of the church. Father Lutz succeeded

Father Hamilton and left the diocese and was pastor for years of a church in New York City. The roof was barely on the walls of the edifice when Father Wheeler became pastor. He was a graduate, also, of the college in Dublin, a classmate of Mr. Donnelly there and afterwards at the Barrens. His estimate of Mr. Donnelly as a student was of the very highest order. He visited Father Donnelly at Independence. In a letter to the St. Louis News-Letter in 1847 while he was West, speaking of Father Donnelly he said: "I was free to say even to the Archbishop that it was an injustice to Father Donnelly to send him outside of civilization, for there is not a priest in the arch-diocese as well equipped mentally as he. He is an omnivorous reader and conversant with several languages, besides his grace and aptitude for church ceremonial have properly kept him before the public eye as Master of Ceremonies Sunday after Sunday and during Holy Week at the Cathedral, at the laying of corner-stones of St. Mary's, St. Patrick's and St. Joseph's Churches, at ordinations, consecrations, and church dedications. He will be lost in the land of the Indian and the rude trapper. Besides his manners are courtly and suited for the culture and refinement of a city."

In his "Recollections of Twenty-five Years in St. Louis," Father Wheeler in July, 1869, speaking again of Father Donnelly, says: "In my letters about a western town in 1847 I wrote that Father Donnelly was intellectually and socially too refined a priest for work among Indians and trappers. I now say of him that, like St. Paul, he is all things to all men. While educated and distinguished in manner he can and has worked like the tireless apostle he is. What a bishop he would be! The East or the West would be equally proud of him."

The morning of his ordination Father Donnelly was appointed pastor of Independence, Jackson County, Missouri. His Grace readily granted the young priest's request to spend a week with the pastor of Old Mines, Missouri. He lost no time in hiring a horse to convey him to the mission of his old friend. His Reverence knew a horse to see him, but never had owned a horse. When he rode behind a horse someone else held the lines. The horse he bargained for was tall and not over-fed, and perhaps it was hunger that made him skittish. There were marks on sides and hips that looked as if they had been worn into the skin by rubbing against fences and trees. The newly ordained asked many questions of the stableman before even approaching the saddle. The answers he received were not assuring. "Yes, the horse had run away in his time, and had unseated his riders on a few occasions, but it was the awkwardness of the mounts rather than the perversity of the animal. This 'hoss' is all right, take my word for it." "Couldn't you give your word to the horse to treat me as square as I'll treat him?" said His Reverence. "All right," came the hostler; then in mock earnestness he whispered to the horse, "This is a good man, you be a good hoss." That was enough. So with a lift from the horseman Father Donnelly was soon mounted, but not easy at all. Then came the starting that was satisfactory at least to the man in the saddle. The horse's head, with the helping hand of his attendant, was directed southward, for Old Mines lay in a southwest direction. Father Donnelly was beginning to feel at comfort and had just said to himself, "Why, horseback riding isn't such a difficult thing as I was led to believe," when a hatless boy rider with a halter for a bridle passed Father Donnelly's horse like a shot, but not too swiftly to give the rented animal a blow with a stick he held in his free hand.   The priest's recollection was that his hat flew from his head, his body began to rise and fall upon the saddle, the stirrups slipped from his feet, and the world around appeared to flee backwards with the velocity of a falling star.   Passers-by stopped and laughed and shouted—he could hear but did not deign a reply.   The moment came as it always comes when a horse is running away at breakneck speed with a green rider; the horse gave a sudden jolt, and the Father felt he was in the air, and in less than a second was sure he was on the hard earth.   It was not his head that made the connection, and the shock of the fall did not rob him of consciousness.   He was alone, fortunately with no scoffer in sight, and that was something if not a consolation.   A first, then a second effort to rise, and he was on his feet.   He felt he was pale, he knew he was in pain.   There were a few rents in his brand-new suit, and his black garments were covered with dust from much-ground macadam.   The horse—well, he was out of sight. Father Donnelly was gifted with the vocabulary of his countrymen and admitted that he did not send blessings after the uncanny fiend.   Then the hat.   His idea of time and distance was very vague just then.   What was the use of going back to search?   It might be a mile or more to the north; it might have been five minutes or half an hour ago since the hat deserted him.   Backwards had no happy recollections, so he would go right ahead.   It was not long until he recognized the old-fashioned cottages of Carondelet.   He directed his steps to the home of Father Saulnier.   Father Saulnier was a jolly old soul and received the young priest with a hearty laugh and told his own

experience of many years with horses. He told
Father Donnelly that he would send out messen-
gers to find the runaway horse, but Donnelly said,
"No, I don't want to lay my eyes on the villain."
After much persuasion he was prevailed on to
spend the night with the venerable missionary.
Early next morning Father Saulnier hired a slow-
going animal and Donnelly proceeded on his way.
When asked how he fared with the second venture his reply was: "One horse story at a time is
enough." He reached his destination, but the
very day after his arrival a letter from the Bishop,
expressing regret that he had to interfere with
his pleasant visit, told him to come immediately
to St. Louis and take the first boat for Independence. Father Thomas Burke and another Lazarist
Father were awaiting him in his new mission.
They were in Independence and felt they ought
to stay there until his arrival. They had many
things to tell him about the territory which his
mission covered.

Some months previously the bishop had requested Father Burke and his Lazarist companion
to visit southwest Missouri from the Arkansas line
to what is now the line dividing Oklahoma and
Missouri, and north to the Kaw River, and east
to a point running south from Lexington. He instructed them to find Catholics and report to him
where resident pastors might be located. To the
Lazarists this was not such a long and unusual
journey, accustomed as they were to go on horseback from the Barrens to Texas and from one end
of that extensive country to the other. Father
Timon and companions, and his predecessors,
made the journey frequently. They were the missionaries in Texas during the forties and fifties,
as the Jesuits were missionaries at the same time
in the district now covered by western Missouri

and eastern Kansas.   Father Burke gave a full
report of the conditions in the vast area he and
his companion traversed.   Independence and Deepwater were selected for residences for pastors.
Deepwater did not receive its pastor as early as
did Independence.   This appointment ended the
missionary duties of the Jesuits in this region.

Father Donnelly did not lose a moment in obey-
ing the orders to start for his new home and his
first work as a priest.   Such a parish, if you will!
Only the two Lazarists could tell him what it physically looked like.   Father Burke prided himself on
being a man of common sense devoid of poetic con-
ceptions, and what he told Father Donnelly about
his new charge was in very plain language and in
no way laudatory of the mountain scenery, limpid
streams and good sized cataracts in his mission.   He
no doubt recommended a few lessons in horseback
riding and suggested some helpful liniments to ease
pain and remove bruises.   He surely did not omit
recommending a convenient and capacious style of
saddle bags and the warmest make of blankets.
Matches had come from inventors and manufaturers
in the far East in 1827 and were not looked upon
acceptably this side of the Mississippi.   The steel
and flint stone would make sparks enough to burn
wet wood—matches might catch fire in one's pocket,
the western pioneers said.   He would require buck-
skin gloves extending to the elbow, boots that would
reach to the knees, a heavy fur cap with lapels to
cover the ears.   The face and nose were to remain
exposed to the blasts from the Rockies and what
were called the "gentle zephyrs" of the prairies, and
when frozen were to be rubbed with snow or ice
until they became sensible to touch and returned to
natural color.   "Put aside the tall hat; the wild looking people out here might shoot holes through it, and
the Indians might take you for a wicked and de-

signing American medicine man.   You'll travel many
a day to take in your great district.   The air out
here is very appetizing, and you will be able to eat
anything put before you.   Keep yourself in the
friendship of God and like St. Patrick the very
snakes will run away from you.   As you are a canny
North of Ireland man, take it from me, you'll give
more out here then you'll ever get."

CHAPTER IV.

HIS PARISH.

BEFORE departing for St. Louis, Father Burke handed the new pastor the latest map of Missouri and with lead pencil marked out his parish. The extent of the parish we may estimate in square miles. The annual Catholic Church Directory states that the diocese of Kansas City, Missouri, covers 23,539 square miles. Deduct about one-third, which seems too much, allowing for the counties of Lafayette and all directly south, and you see the vast space Father Donnelly had to traverse. Lafayette had a pastor at Lexington whose mission went directly south of his county down to Arkansas. Father Donnelly was commissioned to look after the spiritual wants of Catholics in the balance of the territory of the present Kansas City diocese. In a communication to the Catholic Banner dated April, 1879, Father Donnelly touches on his interview with Father Burke. He wrote:

"Dear Catholic Banner: I was appointed pastor of Independence in 1845 within a few hours after my ordination. I asked Bishop P. R. Kenrick if I might spend a few days with an old friend and companion of early days, the pastor of Old Mines. The permission was granted and I left that very afternoon. The next day after my arrival at Old Mines a letter came from the bishop telling me to return to St. Louis without delay and take the first boat westward for Independence. It was Father T. Burke, C. M., who after months of riding over southwest Missouri, wrote Bishop Kenrick that Independence would make a center from which a pastor might radiate to all points from the Kaw River to Arkansas and from the parish of Lexington to the west

line of Missouri. A soldier never responded quicker
to the command of his General than did I. My return was speedier and safer than my journey of a
few days previous. It was under the guidance of my
reverend friend, the pastor of Old Mines. With another Lazarist priest, Father Burke was to wait my
coming at Independence. Instead he met me at
Kanzas as I got off the boat. Father B. was one
of my professors at the Barrens. He handed me
a large map of Missouri with my parish cleverly
drawn out in ink. I had learned before my ordination that Father B. was on a tour of investiga-
tion by order of the bishop. 'Here,' said he, pointing out Independence, 'you are resident pastor,'
then touching the point marked Kanzas, 'this will be
one of your missions for the present, at least.' Then
a third round mark or dot: 'Here is Deepwater—
this will be your third mission. And your fourth
mission—will be the balance of Missouri down to
Arkansas and west to the Territory.' I asked him
about the church at Independence. 'There is no
church or a house for you—that's what you are sent
here for, to build them. There is some property for
a church willed by Bishop Rosatti.' This encouraging information was given me as we sat in a room
of the only hotel in Kanzas."

The few days Father Burke remained were
made helpful for the new pastor. Father Burke had
experience as a traveling missionary in Texas and
had done parish work at the Barrens and at Cape
Girardeau, and as far south as New Madrid. He
was gifted with a hard practical mind and emphatic
views. He had a trite saying that he frequently repeated: "The only college I ever graduated in was
the College of Common Sense." Father Donnelly
on application would have been entitled to a degree
in the same college.

For some little time Father Donnelly was busy trying to solve a problem never suggested by the Lazarist. Father Donnelly was a man at this period advanced in his forties. The great struggle from boyhood was not how to master his studies but how to make life easy for his beloved father and mother. He knew the world and its selfishness much better than did Father Burke who had a home and comfort in every house of his community the world over. If he had been fortunate enough to save any money from his earnings abroad and his salary in America his mind must have been at rest as he saw what was before him. If his fare from St. Louis to Independence had been advanced by his bishop, it was as much as the diocese could afford.

When Bishop Kenrick took charge of his western see he found the new cathedral very much involved in debt. He called the Catholics of the city to a meeting, read a statement of the financial encumbrance, and asked that they would at least reduce the indebtedness. His appeal was met with silence. Not one cent was contributed. This was in 1843. St. Louis was largely Catholic then. Mullanphy, Chouteau, Soulard, Provenchere, Biddle, Lucas, Hunt, and many other wealthy men attended the called meeting. Owners of steamboats and the heads of the trapping and fur industries from St. Louis to the headwaters of the Missouri, bankers, merchants, judges of the courts, and men rich in hundreds of acres of land in and around St. Louis were there but they had nothing to offer.

In what ratio would Catholic generosity show itself beginning at St. Louis and going westward to Independence? At no time was Father Donnelly what might be called sanguine, except in the belief of Kansas City's coming greatness. The few

years at the Barrens and in the St. Louis Seminary
were the only periods of his life when he lived
night and day in the companionship of others. He
was never lonesome when by himself. He would
go to work without delay. Work solves life's
greatest puzzles in war and peace, in fortune making, and in building up great enterprises. He
rented a room from a Catholic family named Gilson. There was no church or home awaiting him
at Independence. The Catholics there did not ask
for a resident pastor; they were satisfied with the
services of religion given at intervals by the Jesuit
missionaries from the Territory. Father Donnelly
quickly grasped his opportunities in his two little
villages. In Kansas City with its come day, go
day, people, and in Independence with its more
stable population, he saw a sample of the same
western lack of generosity experienced by the
bishop in his appeal at St. Louis. The Apostles
began the great work of God among men without
any visible gratuities, but the Apostles built no
churches, schools, or parish houses. The new
Christians threw gold at the feet of Peter and
Paul, but it is to be believed that gold was not in
large quantities—just enough to support them and
pay their expenses going from place to place. But
pondering on conditions would never accomplish
what was before him, and Father Donnelly started
out to beg money from Catholics and non-Catholics
with which to buy property for a cemetery and
build the necessary structures for the parish.
Business men and property holders in new towns
have an ambition to see their home cities grow and
are willing to help on in any way to that end. A
church attracts the passerby. It is a sign of pros-
perity and presages a future for the new settlement.
A school is looked for when one is traveling to make
a new home for himself and family. The years

1845 and 1846 saw a tide of population flowing westward. The Mexican trade had a starting place from Independence and Kansas City to New Mexico. The Santa Fe Trail was opening. Teams of oxen were tugging along with tons of merchandise for the far Southwest and the Rocky Mountains. Returning conveyances with cargoes of Mexican wares were passing east for purchasers in St. Louis and points farther east and south. Nearly all these western commodities were unloaded on steamboats at the landings at Kansas City and at Shelby Landing, a few miles east and south of Independence. Father Donnelly saw his opportunity. He pleaded everywhere and from everybody. Property for a church was willed by Bishop Rosatti. His church was soon purchased. It was a frame building, 24 by 36 feet, which had been erected for a wagon shop, and cost $250.00. The graveyard of ten acres was next acquired; a residence for the pastor quickly followed; and then the great object of his heart, a school house, made the parish complete. He did not wait for a school building to look after the training of his little children, for he used the church for a school. Out of his many cares, Father Donnelly gave the school several hours every day. He was the first teacher as well as the first pastor of Independence. He soon introduced into the new school building a highly competent teacher, Miss Mullins, a sister of the leading merchant at Independence Landing.

Arrivals from the East in most instances came by way of steamboats which landed them at Kanzas. A few left the boats at Shelby Landing, near Independence. Independence is the county seat of Jackson County, which was made a county of the State of Missouri in 1827. The seal of the City of Independence harks back to those days. The design shows four mules attached to the covered wagon or

prairie schooner used in the Santa Fe trade. Caravans for the long journey across the plains were
outfitted and organized at Independence. These
wagons, of the Conestoga pattern, were manufactured first at Pittsburgh, Pennsylvania, and later
at Independence. They were covered with canvas
tightly stretched over hickory bows. Six, eight,
and even ten mules drew these vehicles in the early
days, but after 1829, when Major Riley employed
oxen in transporting baggage and supplies for his
soldiers, the oxen were found to possess greater advantages for this kind of work and gradually replaced the mules. The Santa Fe trade increased
through the years, but after the Mexican War Independence saw with dismay that Westport was becoming the assembling place for the caravans by
reason of its convenience to the steamboats which
landed at the foot of Main Street in Kansas City,
where a ledge of limestone projected out against
the deep water. To regain her prestige Independence built a railroad from her public square to the
Missouri River, to induce steamboats to land and
unload and so cut off the river trade at Kansas City.
This was the first railroad west of the Mississippi
River. It connected the river traffic with the over-
land wagon routes. The rush of Kentuckians, Tennesseeans, and people from the other southern states
into the newly opened Jackson County ended at the
Blue River. Very few went into the Kaw district
where the town of Kanzas was striving for an existence. The trapper, the hunter, the voyageur from
Trois Rivieres, the French-Indian Canadians, with
the few merchants buying and selling, made a distinct and separate community. Kanzas was very
small and looked like an impossible site for a city—
indeed, outside the range of possibility for a future
greatness. People with teams could find no room
in the little front or levee for themselves and their

wagons, and in a circuitous way around the river
bend or through one steep earth road leading south
and east, they headed for Independence, which afforded a large plateau, to rest. Taverns and stables
sprang up to meet the demands in Independence.
The merchants at Kanzas hailed the daily boats,
sold the passengers all they needed for themselves,
and oxen, mules and horses, then directed them to
Independence where those same merchants owned
the taverns and hotels and boarding houses. They
had their warehouses on the Kanzas levee and owned
the one or two banks. Kanzas had every necessity
for the westward-bound except resting accommoda-
tions. The travelers went as directed. They had
to wait at Independence until the government gave
them permits to travel west or south. Those permits were handed them when Uncle Sam could afford a relay of soldiers to protect them over prairie
and mountain and through hostile Indian bands.
The Indians saw their doom at the approach of the
cry "Westward Ho!" Independence boomed while
this condition obtained.

Father Donnelly received many favors for
church and school. He dealt fairly with the mission
at Kanzas and solicited for the demands that would
soon confront him there. The future for him and
his work directed him to the port of entry near the
Kaw, the place where enterprise was evident. He
was Pastor-Resident of Independence, but its day
could not last. That city where energy and commerce were in the ascendant would rule, while
boarding places and enforced resting places would
sink into obscurity as neighboring towns. In the
height of his prognostications he caught at his
breath, when news reached him that a Father Saulnier was appointed resident pastor of Kanzas. Perhaps it was thought at St. Louis that Father Donnelly's energies were sufficiently taxed with the

labors of Independence and his annual visits
through the south and west of his larger territory.
Father Saulnier did not try to live in the little log
resting rooms. He rented a comfortable four-room
cottage near the river landing. He then opened a
school in the log church and was its teacher. Jackson County was then the happy possessor of two
schools, the one under Father Donnelly at Independence, and the other at Kanzas. Father Saulnier, a zealous priest originally from Canada, stuck
close to his teaching and parish duties along the
river front and on the west bottoms and the hill
tops. His Canadian parishioners and a few Catholics from Kentucky liked him, but not enough to
support him; anyhow, his abode in Jackson County
was short. Possibly he thought when he came
West his work would be among the Indians. He
sought no help among those outside of his own
Faith. Father Saulnier returned to Canada.

For the second time Father Donnelly was left
to look after the Catholics on the Missouri River
east of the Kaw River. He was determined to keep
a very close eye on the City of Destiny. With a
light heart and renewed energy he once more took
Kanzas under his care. In 1853 the inhabitants of
Kanzas organized themselves into a city. They
drew up a charter, elected a mayor, council, marshal and judge. Corporate limits were drawn, with
Broadway on the west, Troost Avenue on the east,
the river on the north and Independence Avenue
on the south. Father Donnelly had been one of
the first to advocate the organization of a city. He
was present at the many meetings called for this
purpose and on each occasion made a strong appeal
to throw aside township limitations and become a
city with a charter. The strongest objection to the
movement was the physical condition. Except for
the narrow strip of ground skirting the river, bluffs

as high as little mountains were immediately to the south and west. The few hundred inhabitants were merchants, teamsters, trappers and fishermen, constantly coming and going, and nearly all living in the west and east bottoms. The property owners were willing to assess themselves to pay for all necessary improvements. But where were they to find the contractors? There were no hardy shovelers to tear down the hills and fill up the valleys on the west. Father Donnelly at the public meetings met the difficulty by asking to be deputed to do so and he would bring hundreds of Irishmen from the East to dig and level off and make streets and curb them, and construct sewers. He also guaranteed he would have two men, friends of his at St. Louis, who would build a gas factory and lay gas pipes to bring light to homes and streets. They joyfully accepted his help. He immediately wrote the Boston Pilot and Freeman's Journal of New York asking his countrymen to come to the rescue. He offered them better wages than they could obtain in the East and promised to pay their way to Kansas City. He asked for 150 men from New York and 150 more from Boston. He put his guarantees of good faith in the hands of trustworthy employment agencies in the two eastern cities. He made his offer in time to get the laborers here on the first boats leaving St. Louis in the early spring. He put a wise condition in his contract. He insisted that all the men be from the same county in Ireland. The readers who may recall one of the greatest drawbacks to Irish laborers at that time will recognize the shrewdness of the priest in this demand. He might have made application by way of St. Louis, but the Irish laborers there were not so numerous and were satisfied with their employment and were busy unloading boats and in construction work on the new railroads going north, south and west of St. Louis, and coming through Illinois to reach St. Louis.

When the 300 men arrived it was plain the eastern agencies had been careful in selecting and forwarding willing, husky fellows, and every one from the Province of Connaught. Father Donnelly interviewed them and was more than pleased to learn that they had to a man labored on public works since their arrival in America. He then insisted that every man pledge himself to abstain from liquor, at least while employed in Kansas City. With this they immediately complied. He had not forgotten his good work in Father Matthew's cause in Liverpool. Comfortable quarters for sleeping and eating were awaiting them. They were temporary one-story buildings facing what is now Sixth Street and running from Broadway to the present Bluff Street. Two Catholic families took the contract to feed the men and keep their quarters tidy. In deference to their part of Ireland, their immediate district was dubbed Connaught Town. Father Donnelly was attentive to their wants and their ways. He kept a strict watch on them, seeing that they attended Mass and their religious duties most regularly. As he said one Mass in Kanzas every Sunday they had opportunities to attend the divine service and approach the Sacraments. When the hills were torn away and other work done some of them remained in Kansas City; others went west or found employment on farms, or faced eastward.

CHAPTER V.

FATHER DONNELLY AND THE TEN ACRES.

THE growth of Catholics made Father Donnelly think of a new and larger church edifice. But an unexpected move on the part of his parishioners set back the very thought of building. Father Donnelly's keen eye and observing manner failed him for once. He had a way of finding out what people were thinking about. He was not a mind reader but he was of a shrewd and inquiring turn. He was forever surmising and asking questions. He noticed the people whispering as they gathered in little knots on the church ground on Sundays. He soon learned that secret meetings were being held at a large storehouse owned by a prominent Catholic. He started around making inquiries. The plot was divulged. They were getting signatures for a petition to Archbishop Kenrick asking him to sell the ten acres and two little buildings on the property and with the proceeds purchase a fifty-foot lot with a one-story empty storeroom down in the city. The storeroom was larger than the church they were using. The location was Second and Cherry Streets, adjoining the Chouteau home. He did not display any feeling of opposition, but said the idea was not a bad one. When would they hold their next meeting? He would like to be present; indeed, he thought he would sign the petition. His name would lend strength to the request. He came in from Independence to be with them at the next meeting. The attendance was large and representative of the parish. Mr. P. Shannon, a prominent merchant and afterwards mayor of the city, presided. The Jarboes, Chouteaus, Guinotte, Tour-

geon, Troost, and Mr. Payne whose wife was a
Catholic, with many others, were present. Speeches
advocating the object of the meeting were made.
One sentiment ran through the address and was
applauded by clapping of hands; the ten acres
should be traded for the fifty-foot lot. When
everyone anxious to talk had been heard, Father
Donnelly was invited to take the floor. He expressed great pleasure at the large attendance.
It showed the parishioners were interested in the
welfare of the parish. The little hamlet of yesterday is today a city; it must have a church and
this is one of the ways of getting it. "But," he
continued, "I find names absent from the petition.
Be sure and get everyone in the parish to sub-
scribe. There is no particular hurry. Take a few
days more to make a complete list of Catholics."
Father Donnelly was with the meeting as well as
in it. The people had won the pastor. The meeting adjourned. Father Donnelly mounted his Indian pony and went home to Independence. He
immediately wrote a letter to the archbishop telling of the meeting, that he was present and had
signed the petition. "I did so, Your Grace, because
I recognize the shrewdness of the old Irish saying,
'If you can't bate the enemy, jine him.' I beg you
that you keep this letter a secret. You will recall
the ten acres they wish to barter away for a fifty-
foot lot and an unused frame storehouse. Once
before Doctor Troost and other promoters made
the same request to your Grace. Kansas City has
thrown off the appearance of an ungainly but
lively little hamlet. We have dug down big hills
and filled up deep ravines. Our streets are laid
out and macadamized and guttered, and brick sidewalks line each side. We have become citified.
Our Catholics have all of a sudden found out the
church in the ten acres is away off on one of the

few remaining hills. They begin to complain of
the fatigue of climbing, which all at once has
become unbearable. The females of our flock say
that going up to the log church is 'horrid' and that
the streets in the new city are becoming impossible
for shopping on Mondays because of the sticky yellow mud carried down from the church every Sunday. Then, your Grace, some enterprising real
estate men looking for commissions are back of
the movement and have aroused our people. The
other village churches are looking for sites within
the city limits. The city is daily growing in population. The limits laid out in the charter are not
extensive enough. The city must grow south. It
cannot grow north, for the Missouri River is the
north boundary. It must grow south as the trade
is in that direction, and then it must develop a
residence district which will sooner or later be on
the plateau called Westport. Until that time comes
the people will choose the northwest section for
their homes. I predict the ten acres and immediate
neighborhood will be for years the most desirable
residence part of Kansas City. Where the city is
now must necessarily be the business district. Besides, your Grace, selling ten acres for a 50-foot
lot near the levee would be an egregious mistake.
In a little while we would be buying another fifty
feet to enlarge the poorly constructed building there
now, then we would need more property for the
priest's house and school, and it would be a constant patching up and lengthening out, and after
a short time all our parishioners would have moved
to newer and more desirable neighborhoods. Ten
acres consecrated by the memory of Kansas City's
first resident pastor and deeded by him to your
predecessor, Bishop Rosatti, has untold wealth in
its stone deposits and the very clay in it for many
feet down means thousands of dollars when moulded

into brick. The ten acres may yet build a cathedral and institutions of charity and learning. Do not be hard on me if I have been a little foxy in my way of heading off the well meant intentions of my flock."

Father Donnelly completed his remonstrance, and though the hour of midnight had arrived, he saddled his horse and rode rapidly towards Liberty where he awaited the first eastbound steamboat. The postmaster on board the boat received his letter and carried it to St. Louis. The archbishop answered the committee, saying he could not comply with their request. Father Donnelly was happy but not boastful over his success in saving the ten acres. His letter was really prophetic—the most aristocratic part of Kansas City for many years was the immediate neighborhood of the ten acres.

There was merit in at least two of the reasons assigned in the petition. But the reasons strongest to him was the distance for many of the people and the difficulty of getting there. The church was on a bluff looking over the west bottoms and the Missouri and Kaw Rivers. There was a deep ravine south of the church, running to what is Eleventh Street, and growing deeper as it neared Broadway, then taking a course east, skirting the north side of Broadway and making a short turn to Fifth Street. In the rainy season the ravine was impassable except for a very frail-looking bridge near the entrance to the church property This bridge led into the southeast corner of the ten acres. The majority of the people had to face danger from bridge and water. Mr. Shannon, as chairman of the petitioners, received the response from the archbishop. He showed it to Father Donnelly, who suggested that a meeting of the parish at large be held after the Mass on the following Sunday. At the meeting he told the people he had thought of a scheme somewhat similar to their written proposal to his Grace. Instead of exchanging properties, why not rent the store and 50-foot lot near Second and Cherry Streets? "You will have the use of the property there for a nominal sum and still own the ten acres. You will have all the conveniences of the new church and none of the difficulty of coming and going." The suggestion took with the congregation. On the next Sunday, Father said Mass in the frame building in the city, two blocks south of the Missouri and four blocks north from Independence Avenue, the south line or limit of Kansas City. The church held more worshippers and brought out some non-Catholics. The little altar from the old church was there, and the pictures. The hard oak pews, not even planed, were substituted by shining pine ones which were painted before the second Sunday. It was told by many people that Father Donnelly preached much better in the rented church. "We carted down everything we could except the bell and the name. Father Le Roux never christened his little log church, calling it simply a church, in his transfer of title to Bishop Rosatti. I had in my mind a name most sacred to me from earliest days, which would soon be the title of an article of Faith."

It was the sale of portions of the ten acres that practically built the present cathedral. It was the sale of the west half of the block on which the cathedral stands that erected the St. Joseph Orphan Asylum. The stones quarried from the asylum site were formed into the footing courses and range work as well as the window and door sills and steps to the front and rear entrances of the building. Father Donnelly out of his own means paid the expenses up to the brick work. The second attempt to dispose of the original church was foiled.

A few years and the city limits had to be extended. The river neighborhood was given over to business and the many residents who could afford it moved to higher and newer points. The words of Father Donnelly were verified in his own day, the old church neighborhood was known as Quality Hill, where the wealthy erected homes that would do credit to the best in St. Louis and the eastern cities. Father Donnelly looked with watchful eyes upon the ten acres. They were to him like a sacred inheritance, and inheritances are sometimes disputed.

After the Civil War the city limits kept spreading from the first charter size. Ten acres of ground daily growing more valuable looked to the Kansas City Catholics like a fortune does to wishful, waiting heirs while the grandsire lives long beyond the years allotted man. The city's growth and the increased number of Catholics justified another parish. St. Patrick's was founded in 1869. Father James Halpin and his congregation held services in the basement of a nearby unfinished German church named for Saints Peter and Paul. The new parish looked promising. Its people were largely new arrivals. They wanted a church. The city had not yet moved southward. The tendency was east. Main Street was the division line, and from Main Street east and west there was an elevation of many feet, beginning south of Eighth Street. The new pastor, Father Halpin, had just left the Society of Jesus where he had been a professor for many years. At the very first business meeting in the new parish the question raised was not how much will each one give to the new parish, but how much of the ten acres are we entitled to? A committee was appointed to wait on Father Donnelly and make a claim on what they maintained was theirs. The ten acres were again a bone of contention. Father

Donnelly's response was a letter from Archbishop Kenrick, which he read them. He introduced the letter by saying: "I knew you were coming." This letter, like all Archbishop Kenrick's letters, was very short and to the point.

"Rev. B. Donnelly,
Rev. Dr. Sir:

"In answer to yours of Nov. 20, I wish to say, the 10 acres belong to Immaculate Conception parish. The coming new parish, as well as all coming parishes, shall have no claim on the site purchased by my predecessor, Bishop Rosatti, from Fr. Le Roux. Yours in Christ.

†P. R. Kenrick."

This letter headed off all further demands on the ten acres. A storm of indignation came from the disappointed claimants which finally subsided and was followed by a wholesome spirit of rivalry. Father Donnelly treasured the letters he received in the instance of the early committee, and this blank refusal to Father Halpin. He would read these letters to coming new pastors to warn them against any aggressions, and would say, "You see what you may expect."

The new parish witnessed the German congregation insisting on a parish graveyard. This was a tolerated privilege demanded and enjoyed everywhere the German Catholics started a parish. St. Patrick's parish persisted in its clamor for a cemetery of its own. Father Halpin was succeeded by Father Archer, who, after a short while, was appointed to St. Patrick's Church, St. Louis. Father Dunn was the third pastor. He agreed with his people that a parish graveyard was right and proper. Father Donnelly's letter of protest brought a response from the archbishop forbidding any other graveyard for the English-speaking parishes than the one in the original ten acres.   He also stated that the control of that cemetery would remain in the hands of Father Donnelly.   Before this letter from the archbishop arrived Father Dunn had been deeded several acres for his parish cemetery.   The present came from a prominent member of Father Donnelly's parish.   Of course, the new site was never used for the purpose of the transfer.

The 2nd and Cherry Street Church served its purpose well—there was quiet in the parish except for the usual grumblers who refused to contribute their share in paying the rent of the 50-foot lot and the church.   Father Donnelly observed that some of his people who had homes near the rented property were disposing of them and purchasing near Broadway and not far from the old original property.   Business was encroaching.   He satisfied himself that the ten acres near 12th Street had ideal soil for brickmaking.   He made test after test and then with the help of two brickmakers from St. Louis he began the manufacture of brick. He claimed his was the first large brickyard ever opened in Kansas City.   Several business houses and many residences were constructed of his product.   Bricks of course commanded a good price, but lumber cost more because it had to be shipped a great distance from the East.   Kansas was a vast prairie.   The industries in St. Joseph, Liberty, Weston and Lexington, all neighboring and larger towns than Kansas City, were tobacco and hemp factories.   Negro slaves were the workmen. Forming materials for buildings must have been exclusively in the hands of white men, and the native white man that was forced to work in the slave states selected an occupation that afforded him plenty of time to lounge.

Father Donnelly's Church, Broadway between Eleventh and Twelfth Streets. Built in 1856; torn down in 1885

When his brickyard was under way, Father Donnelly worked for hours daily side by side with his help. The venture was a paying one and he soon had money enough in the local banks to justify him in proclaiming in newspaper and church and to the citizens as he met them that he would soon start on a new brick church. The bricks were on hand, the stone for the foundation and trimmings were near the site of the coming structure and the location would face Broadway on the ten acres. The glitter from the new city had dimmed and people were looking for building places that would give ample room and the comforts of air and sunshine, just a little outside corporation lines. A city narrowed down like Kansas City was certain to be dusty and smoky. Grass and trees fade and die from smoke and dust off streets. The ten acres, free from the trampling of people for a few years, were carpeted with a verdure of blue grass planted with the best Kentucky seed. The trees were well kept. Outside of the four acre portion alloted to the cemetery the grounds were converted into a shaded park with seats and walks. The old church property became a popular visiting place on Sundays and holidays. What a delightful site for a church! How pleased the people were at the prospect of soon coming back to the first location! Father Donnelly had won again, and this was a victory —he was leading his flock home again!

Father Donnelly resumed his letters to the Boston Pilot and the New York Freeman's Journal after the arrival of the 300 laborers to tear down the bluffs and small mountains and fill up the valleys and hollows made by the rains and springs on their way to the Missouri and Kaw Rivers. Many desirable families heeded his advice and came west, some of them to make their homes in Kansas City and others to farm in Jackson County and in Kansas. The growth of Catholics in and close to Kansas City demanded a new church. He had money on hand from collections and from the sale of bricks made on the ten acres and of stone taken out of the property, and of lime from the two lime kilns he had in operation for months. With the archbishop's permission he started on the excavations. The footing courses were soon in place and the stone ranges went up quickly. The date of the cornerstone laying was the second Sunday after Pentecost, 1856. The ceremony attracted a very large attendance. Boat excursions brought people from Liberty and Weston, from St. Joseph, and a company of soldiers from Fort Leavenworth. It would seem that everybody in Independence and Kansas City turned out. Father Hammil came all the way from Lexington and brought many people with him. From St. Louis came Fathers William Wheeler, Patrick O'Brien, and the venerable Father Saulnier, the priest whom Father Donnelly visited on his way to Old Mines the day of his ordination. Two Jesuit Fathers from St. Mary's, Kansas, kindly gave their presence. Father O'Brien preached the sermon and Father Donnelly laid the cornerstone. The size of the edifice was 30 by 60 feet. The walls were of brick, made and carefully selected by the pastor and his helpers in his parish brickyard.

Father Donnelly was ready to entertain his reverend guests. East of the new cornerstone he had just completed a two-story house for a residence. In his reveries—and he was forever planning and looking ahead—he could see himself comfortably ensconced in the largest brick pastoral residence west of St. Louis, a few feet from the largest and the best put-together church between the Kaw and Mississippi Rivers. But how

men's dreams "gang aft agley!"   Father Donnelly pushed on the church structure without any
unnecessary delay.   In early summer he dedicated
the church.   The dedication sermon was delivered
by Bishop Miege, Vicar-Apostolic of Kansas, who
also performed the dedication ceremonies.   During all this labor Father Donnelly would steal away
to Independence perhaps three times a week.   He
was resident pastor of Independence and simply
missionary priest at Kansas City.   It would sound
better and be in keeping with Canon titles to call
his Kansas City church a "chapel of ease," a succursal church.   He did not give the name of a
saint to the chapel on 5th Street, and he tells in a
letter to the Catholic Banner that it was Father
De Smet who christened the unnamed log church St.
Francis Regis.   On the day of dedication, before
Bishop Miege began the ceremonies, Father Donnelly, standing on the altar, announced: "This
church will be dedicated to the Virgin Mother
under the title of Immaculate Conception."   By
that title the bishop dedicated it, by that title it
was known and called by bishops, priests and people, and when the first bishop of Kansas City
dedicated his cathedral he announced to the vast
congregation, "I now take the name Mary Immaculate from the little church near by and hand it
over to our new cathedral.   Let it be called Immaculate Conception Cathedral."   The writer was
present in the sanctuary the day of the dedication of the cathedral and heard these words of the
bishop, and preached the dedication sermon.

CHAPTER VI.

MRS. DILLON'S RECOLLECTIONS OF EARLY DAYS.

At the suggestion of the writer, in 1878, Mrs. Dillon, Kansas City's oldest native resident, wrote her recollections of the early days for publication in the Catholic Banner. Her account follows:
Editor of Catholic Banner:

I cheerfully comply with your request to write about myself and early Kansas City for your newspaper. I have the proud distinction of being the first white child born on the site of Westport. I never heard of any Indian child born before me here and so I presume I am the very first child of any kind or race born here. Indians may have and no doubt did pass back and forth but never pitched their tents in these parts. The Indians, like the first white men, lived close to streams for the same reason the whites did—because it was easier of ingress and egress, and because they found food in the fishes that were in the Kansas and Missouri Rivers. They hunted on the plains where the buffaloes and other wild animals were in abundance. The soil was productive, so they had plenty to eat.

My parents came from Kentucky. They lived for a little while after their arrival on the bottom land near the Kaw known as the West bottoms, to distinguish it from the bottoms east, or East bottoms. The West bottoms were held in preference by newcomers, because they faced on two rivers. One day my father strayed over the big bluffs and after a few miles' walk southward came to the high level known now as Westport. On his return he told Mother that the place he had visited was more desirable for a home as it was much cooler and was away from the damp fogs of the streams, and the soil reminded him of Kentucky. The low lands were sandy. Besides in his native state he had lived near the Ohio River and on two different occasions was driven out of his home by high water floods. On his walk south he found two Kentucky families who advised him strongly to come out near them and they would help him cut down trees and build a log cabin. Mother assented and next day they put their few belongings in their wagon and drove south. They were kindly received, and the very next day set to work cutting the timber. Within a week, with the help of their neighbors, they had their small log house ready for occupation. It was one-story and 8x12 feet in size. It was in this log cabin I was born on March 25th, 1820. The ground was no man's land, my parents were told; it was in territory ceded some little time before to the United States by the Osage Tribe of Indians. Father never gave a thought to ownership nor preemption nor squatter's right—just took possession. Our two neighbors were equally careless about title. Another way to acquire property at that time was by government patent, but they knew nothing about patents from Uncle Sam.

It was easy to keep the home warm, for wood was plentiful. But the larder had to be provided for. In the West bottoms the Astor Fur Company needed food and lodging for their employees and the Canadian-French were making more than a living feeding and rooming the hunters and trappers and selling garden products to the fur boats and to men passing in skiffs north and south. Nature had made a good landing place or levee between the West and East bottoms. And soldiers on their way to the Fort Leavenworth would go to the Canadian squatters for potatoes, chickens and prairie birds, and sometimes make contracts for a regular supply for the army. Money was passing hands and a few stores were doing good business. There was some stir in the bottoms and my parents were soon forced by a constantly thinning out of their purse to leave their new home and go back to the sandy soil they had recently left. Our Canadian friends welcomed us back. They told my parents that a Catholic priest from Florissant had promised to visit them and administer the consolations of religion. "Oh," said they to Mother, "there are many little children who will be baptized when he comes." It was in 1821, early in spring, he arrived. His name was Father La Croix.

During my parents' stay here before going to what is now Westport, a goodly number of our neighbors would go to the home of Peter Clement Lessert every Sunday to recite Catholic prayers, in lieu of Mass, for up to the coming of Father La Croix no priest had ever visited here. My parents were very friendly with their Canadian neighbors and went every Sunday to the prayer meeting. Father and Mother at that time were not affiliated to any church. Their neighbors were good, simple people and their church had made them such. It did not require much persuasion to induce my parents to consent to have my brother, three years of age, and me, their baby, baptized by Father La Croix. He remained here about a month. Mass and other services were held in the home of Clement Lessert. Before Father left here for St. Joseph my parents were baptized by him. My Godparents were Callis Montardeau and his wife Helois. The date of my baptism was May 14th, 1821. Father La Croix spent some weeks in and around St.

Joseph and then went north to the Sioux country—
it was called by that name and is now Sioux City.
He returned to west bottoms in the fall and said
Mass two Sundays.   This time the Mass was said
the first Sunday in the home of Peter La Liberte
and the second Sunday in Francois Trumley's residence in tne west bottoms.   The Chouteau family
had not yet arrived and all the Catholics were in
the west bottoms.

The historical data I am now giving you is not
reminiscent, as I was not at a mentally receptive
condition at the time I am mentioning.   I have
before me a diary given me in my tenth year by
my Godmother, Mrs. Montardeau.   She was an educated woman, who before the days of the French
Revolution was a student in one of the best convent
academies in her native France.   Her parents were
killed by the madmen of those days and her property confiscated.   She came out West from Canada.
You asked me for church history.   I find in this
diary or memorandum book that the next priest
who visited this site was Father Joseph Lutz from
the Cathedral at St. Louis.   He made his home
with the Montardeau family.   He was of German
birth but spoke French and English well.   From
the West Kansas bottoms he visited the Kaw and
Kickapoo Tribes.   It was from the Kaw Tribes
Kansas and Kansas City got their names.   They
were nearly all Catholics and were the Indians that
called on Bishop Rosatti for a priest.   Father Lutz
was secretary to Bishop Rosatti and in 1845 built
St. Patrick's Church in St. Louis.   He left St. Louis
and became pastor of a church in New York City,
where he died.   He returned his calls to this place
at intervals as late as the spring of 1844.   I find
in the Montardeau diary that his last appearance
here was in the early spring of 1844.   He left in
time to escape the great flood of 1844.

I often thought over what I heard many a
Catholic mother say when I was a child: "What
a terrible affliction families bring on themselves
by moving into new and distant countries and thus
cutting themselves away from all the benefits and
consolations of religion. The struggle for existence in new parts is nothing nearly so hard as the
feeling, we are bereft of God's best ministrations in
life and death. What a happy news when the word
went around that a priest is coming to us!"

Father Roux came here in 1833. I can recall
his arrival. While here he lived with the Chouteau
family, whose residence then and for many years
was where Cherry and Second Streets meet. He
said Mass in the Chouteau residence every Sunday.
Close to the Chouteaus was a small frame building used by Father Donnelly for church purposes,
when the Catholics tired of climbing up the hills
to the log church.

Father Roux visited here from Kaskaskia on
at least two occasions after leaving this part of
the world. It was Father Roux who purchased the
ten acres and gave them to Bishop Rosatti for a
consideration of two dollars. Father Donnelly held
on to the ten acres with the log church and office
or rest structure nearby. Neither Father Roux
nor any of the succeeding priests ever lived in this
little log affair. It is still standing and is always
called Kansas City's first parsonage, but in fact
never was fitted or occupied by any priest coming,
going, or staying here.

Fathers Van Quickenborne and P. Van Hoecken
passed here on their first visit to the Kickapoo
village in 1836. The memory of the Jesuit Fathers
is as clear to me as events of yesterday. They
lived with the Pottawatomie Indians and attended
here at intervals until the coming of Father Donnelly in 1845. I often heard from Father Donnelly

that it was Father De Smet who gave the name St. Francis Regis to the little log church. You ask me about St. Xavier's Church. There never was any such church here. The one church structure was all required. A church at Westport—let me tell you I was at Mass the Sunday Bishop Kenrick appeared here. I recall he baptized and confirmed before beginning Mass. He put down the names of the baptized and confirmed and requested that the entries be made at the church at Westport. Before taking a boat for St. Louis he was waited on by nearly all the Catholics. Among other things he told us that he wished the baptisms and confirmations done by him the last Sunday be forwarded to the Westport Church. "Westport Church?" said Mr. Chouteau, "There is no such church. Ours is the only church in these parts." "Why," said the Bishop, "I was informed there was a church at Westport, and as there was no priest to receive me here I made the request after writing the names. Where do the Fathers live who attend here?" "Over the line some miles in the Territory," replied Mr. Chouteau. "I am expecting a long visit from a Bishop friend, and shall request him to visit here all through these parts to give me a correct report of churches and missions." A bishop named Barron soon arrived and went west to the Jesuits for some days. Our own bishop seemed displeased to have no priest when he reached here, and said something about "vision churches."

The coming of Father De Smet was always a gala day. Everyone knew and loved him and everybody has heard and read of his many conversions in the Indian tribes. Father Donnelly is a combination of the missionary and the resident priest. He is a man of great versatility and earnestness. He is tanned by the sun, and hardened by the

chill of the winter.   He and his Indian pony are
known from Kansas all through southeast Missouri.

Father Roux was a son of a family of means
abroad. He was not a forceful character, but rather
inclined to be just going to do something.   He
surely did a wise thing when he purchased the ten
acres for the coming church.   Father Roux was
of commanding appearance, with light hair and
refined taste.

Father Saulnier, who was here for a little over
one year, has the credit of starting and teaching
the first school ever in Kansas City.   His stay was
entirely too short.   From Father La Croix, the
first priest, to Father Dalton, the latest arrival, I
have had some acquaintance with everyone.

When I married Mr. Dillon I soon found myself on my native heath, where I was born.   All
during the days of the Santa Fe trail and when
hundreds were traveling to the California and
Pike's Peak gold regions, Westport was a lively
village.   It was all tents and looked like the resting
place of an army.   Few buildings went up.   Nearly
all the arrivals came with tents and lived in them
while waiting for a cavalcade of soldiers for safety
going through the plains and over the mountains.
It seems like yesterday since newly appointed
bishops and their priests would pitch their tents
in and around our town.   They said Mass in the
tents every morning.   Occasionally on a Sunday I
would request a bishop or priest to say his Mass
in my parlor.   At least three times Father Donnelly favored us with Divine Services.   I recall he
always brought one of his nephews to serve his
Mass.

From his arrival, Father Donnelly accommo-
dated himself in many ways to the needs of his
congregation.   He preached a sermon in English.
He was quick in picking up a language, and was

here only a few Sundays when his knowledge of French justified him in delivering a short sermon in French. I know that when he came here he could not converse in French. But he gave us all a surprise one Sunday by saluting a number of Osage Indians who stopped over on their way to Washington. Several weeks before their arrival Father Donnelly learned from his friends, the Jesuit Fathers at Osage, that they were coming. He promptly called on the Professor of Indian Language at Shawnee Mission to teach him the Osage dialect. He repeated his visits and remained for hours every day acquiring enough of the tongue to make a talk to the coming Indians. After a sermon in English he addressed the Indians for fully fifteen minutes in the Osage. They were all attention while he spoke. They did not seem surprised, for Indians never look surprised. After Mass we gathered around the twenty or thirty natives and asked if they understood Father Donnelly. They said, "Yes, he speak Indian." The white man, the government agent, told us that Father Donnelly made himself thoroughly understood. He continued his lessons in Indian for a long while afterwards. The same Indians, on their way home, were here for Sunday and Father Donnelly again addressed them in the Osage tongue.

This is my second venture in newspaper lines. I pray kind indulgence.

MRS. DILLON.

CHAPTER VII

FATHER DONNELLY GIVES UP THE INDE-
PENDENCE PARISH, 1857.

THE dedication of the Kansas City brick church was still fresh in Father Donnelly's recollection and he was in his home at Independence when a priest named Father Denis Kennedy made his appearance and announced himself pastor of Kansas City. If Father Donnelly ever had a nerve he must have turned it off as one turns off an electric light. With extended hand and a friendly smile playing on his face, he congratulated and welcomed the brother priest, and to continue what he considered the pleasantry, he complimented him and said, "By the way, there's not a priest in the diocese that would not be honored by such a promotion." When the visitor was seated Father Donnelly asked him when he had arrived, and had he come by way of Kansas City. "Well, Father Donnelly," he replied, "I came by boat to Kansas City yesterday, and I propose to return on the first eastbound packet. Here is my letter of appointment." Father Donnelly read the letter, witn the ease and self-control of a man who was receiving commonplace news. He said: "Father Kennedy, do not go away. You surely have been promoted. Where you have come has a great future and a good-sized congregation. Central Township, where you were, will never be big enough to act as tail to the kite of St. Louis. Besides, it will not advance your standing with your archbishop to show the white feather now. What is the matter? Why do you refuse Kansas City?" "I learn," said the priest, "there is a debt on the parish and I will never undertake to pay a debt

made by another." "Well," said Father Donnelly,
"I do not want you to go away. Would you take
a parish out here, without a cent of debt, and with
church, school, and property of several acres, and
a cemetery? If you say yes, I'll give you Independence and go myself to Kansas City and pay
off that small debt." Father Kennedy assented
and remained as guest with Father Donnelly until
a response from a letter to Archbishop Kenrick
arrived. The archbishop replied, "I am satisfied
with the arrangement between Fathers Donnelly
and Kennedy, and hereby make the appointments
of Father Donnelly to be resident pastor of Kansas City and Father Kennedy resident pastor of
Independence." Father Donnelly left within a few
hours for his home in Kansas City. He carried
with him a satchel containing absolute necessities,
and a few days afterwards removed his library
and wearing apparel. Father Donnelly, having a
keen business sense, realized he got the better in
the transaction and for that he thanked God and
his own shrewdness.

Father Denis Kennedy was a worthy successor
at Independence. He was gifted with the true
missionary spirit of Father Donnelly. His health
was rugged and he never tired, following Father
Donnelly's long journeys on horseback in search
of the scattered members of the fold of Christ.
During the bushwhacking and guerilla raids by
independent bands of southern cavalry, and the
counterraids of what was called the Jennison Jay-
hawkers from Kansas into Jackson County, Father
Kennedy's services were kindly recognized by the
contending forces. He was frequently sent for by
both sides to administer to the wounded and the
dying. One night on his way to one of these calls
he was suddenly halted and commanded to iden-
tify himself. He gave his name and place of resi-

dence. The outlaw troop had never heard of him.
When he said he was a priest they immediately
connected him with some spies and detectives who
in the garb of ministers of the Gospel were sent to
ferret out the hiding places of Quantrill and his
daring aide-de-camp, Jesse James. They refused
to heed his pleas and ordered him to dismount.
He was led to a convenient tree to be shot. Western
outlaws always prefer to kill a victim when he has
the support of a tree. When the three sharpshoot-
ers who did the executions were moving to the
usual thirty paces in front, a soldier sleeping nearby on the ground suddenly awoke. As he sat up
his eyes fell on the condemned man. The first
glance convinced him he knew the prisoner, and
the second look made him shout: "Boys, don't
shoot. That's a man who harbored me and
Brother Frank in his house in Independence when
we were wounded by the Jennison fiends. That's
Father Kennedy, a Catholic priest." The execu-
tioners lowered their guns. It was Jesse James
who had spoken. He rushed to Father Kennedy
and asked where he was going. "To visit a dying
man," replied the priest. "I thought so," said Jesse,
"you're always good to the sick and wounded and
the dying. I'll escort you, Father, and that fellow
that ordered you shot will go along, too. That's
Bill Sheppard, a pretty bad fellow, but he isn't
afraid of anything or anybody. Come on, Bill!"
ordered the superior officer, Jesse James. They
rode side by side of the priest to the home of the
dying Catholic. They then saw Father Kennedy to
his door in Independence. This story was frequently told by Father Kennedy after the war.
Two of Father Kennedy's parishioners became as-
sociated with the Quantrill guerilla band, as they
were called, and in an interview with the reporter
of a Kansas City evening paper, said they heard

the occurrence related by those who were with
Jesse on the night that Father Kennedy had the
close call.   Father Kennedy was transferred to
Hannibal, Missouri, in 1871, and before he died
purchased the church erected by the Congre-
gationalists at Hannibal immediately before the
Civil War.   It is one of the largest and finest
church edifices in Missouri.   Its cost price when
labor and material were low was $70,000.00.

Father Kennedy's successors at Independence
were Father O'Neill, Father Kennedy's predecessor at Hannibal, Father E. J. Shea, a brilliant and
hard working priest, then first assistant to Bishop
Ryan at St. John's Church, St. Louis, who was
appointed pastor when Father O'Neill resigned to
join the diocese of Chicago.   But Father Shea declined the proffer.   Father T. Fitzgerald then became pastor of Independence where he continued
until his death in 1910.

CHAPTER VIII.

COLONIZER AND ENTHUSIAST.

FATHER DONNELLY quickly cleared off the few thousand dollars' indebtedness on the new Immaculate Conception Church. The Kansas City parish did not long confine the labors of Father Donnelly. Shortly after leaving Independence he received orders to attend as outmission the city of Liberty, which meant all Clay County. This new charge, after two years, was transferred to the pastor of Independence. Bishop Miege in 1857 requested Father Donnelly to take care of the handful of Catholics a few miles across the Kaw in the Kanzas Territory. While doing this service for his friend he induced some very desirable Irish families recently from his own county in Ireland to buy farms in Kansas on the road leading to Leavenworth. This settlement was fortunate in following his advice. Their farms were very productive and the purchasers were practical, industrious farmers. Some few, however, never got over their lonesomeness for their old country and were constantly finding fault and regretting their investment. Father Donnelly was always solicitous for his countrymen and aided them in selecting good locations. His choice was the farming lands "The only trade you ever followed at home was farming. Go to the farms," he would say. "The temptations of the cities are great, and too many of you are yielding to them." After his experience with the few discontented ones in Kansas he ever afterwards was slow to point out any particular place for future homes except within his own parish lines.

Father Donnelly's many letters to eastern
newspapers made his name well known in New
York and Boston.   The name of the Kansas settlement was the one usually given every locality entered by Irishmen.   It was called "Irish Settlement."   That name may be frequently found in the
church directories of the '40s and '50s.   For instance, in the Directory of 1849 the Jesuit missionaries from St. Mary's claim a mission called Irish
Settlement, but its whereabouts is not printed.   No
doubt there was such a place which the Fathers
attended.   The U. S. Post Office did not in those
early days have the right of giving the names to
new settlements, or at least did not exercise it.
Chaos is the primitive condition in new countries
and it requires time and the strain of many inconveniences to install the order of civilization.

The many letters to New York and Boston
newspapers made his name well known also along
the Atlantic Coast.   His mail was unusually large
as a result.   To the mechanic he would say: "Stay
where the factories are, go to work at what you
know best.   Farming is not a slipshod undertaking.   A farmer must know the soil and be able to
till it.   Farming is a science, it is an industry that
requires experience, brains, steady habits, a strong
heart ready to meet success without having one's
head turned, able to surmount the uncertainties
that come with weather, drought, and insects, flies
and grasshoppers.   A farmer must be studious,
learning every new method and agricultural in-
vention and being quick in using them.   He must
be sober and never get tired.   Don't come to the
western prairies unless you are ready and willing
to labor in sunshine and storm, in failure and success.   The farmer must be an early riser and con-
serve nature by going to bed early.   If you are
ready to accept all these conditions, come west;

and there are many more chances of success than there are dangers of failure."

The Boston Pilot had a large circulation among the Irish in America. It was extensively read in Ireland also. It had many readers among the priests there. Father Donnelly frequently received letters from the Irish parish priests in relation to homes for their own immediate families and their parishioners contemplating coming to America. The result was that a number of the Irish immigrants of the '50s and '60s took up farms in Jackson and surrounding counties of Missouri. Farm land was cheap, and when guided by Father Donnelly's advice they invariably succeeded. At this day it is not unusual to find the offspring of those pioneers in possession of the original farms with enlarged area, satisfied with conditions and holding sacred the memory of the priest who induced their fathers and grandfathers to acquire western homes. Before Father Donnelly retired from Independence, many of his countrypeople were successful businessmen and rich contractors. Many, very many, Catholics who amassed fortunes in Kansas City were free to say they owed their start and their continued success to the advice and sometimes the help they received from Father Donnelly, or through his influence.

From the very day of his arrival all through his thirty-five years as priest he saw a great future for Kansas City. When it became the gateway for the thousands going West to open up a trade with Mexico by the Santa Fe Trail, when he beheld armies of fortune-seekers wild with the lust of gold in far-off California in 1849, and troopers of the get-rich-quick, leaving farms, machine shops and banks in the quest of the same rich metal at Pike's Peak in 1859, when he saw young men from colleges and universities of Massachusetts and

New York coming to the Kansas prairies and towns to grow up and grow great, like Senator Ingalls, in the West, he would repeat with pleasure his belief in the future of his city. "Everyone who passes through will speak of the natural advantages of the city geographically. Coming or going, the western traveler must pass through Kansas City. The very center of the United States,* by mathematical calculation and by the help of the compass, is within a very few miles of our city. All roads led to Rome—it was the center of the Old World. All roads must and do lead to Kansas City, the geographical center and the coming business center of our country." Newspapers, magazines and illustrated journals were writing up Kansas City, the town that ushers you into the vast plains and the home of the buffaloes. Every arrival left at least some money there and joined in the prediction that Kansas City had a great future. From every boat a few would stop off to make their homes there. Poets and artists would get off the boats to purchase food and tents for a stay on the prairies. From Kansas City through Kansas the vast rolling plains were called prairies. The geographies in the schools and the metropolitan newspapers always said "deserts." There was the great American desert unfolding itself in gentle undulations and rising in altitude until it reached the grade of 9,000 feet above the ocean, where it lost its identity in the foothills of the Rocky Mountains. The literary invaders to the land of the cactus and buffalo-grass and sand entered with the popular idea of the desert. But the popular idea was unlike the thing itself.

*The geographical center of the United States is on a farm ten miles north of Smith Center, Kansas.

The ground was bare and sometimes level, but frequently diversified with hills and valleys. Its sandy bareness, except for occasional tufts of grass that were bristling and brittle, and the effect of sun and cloud, heat and distance, resulted in a perpetual shifting and varying color. By this play of air and sky, its primary tones of red, yellow, blue, dazzling white and dazzling black, were constantly changing into hazes, transparencies, lights and shadows of infinite variety and beauty. It was never monotonous because it was never twice the same. This was Nature at its very best, before commerce built its roads of steel from Kansas City to the Rockies. This was Nature as the poet and artist saw it before civilization dotted it with human habitations and lined it with macadam and asphalt passways. This was the way Nature painted its own canvas, stretching from Missouri to the sublime Rockies. Poets raved over a beauty and sublimity they never saw before and never dreamed of. Kansas City was alive to the opportunities of such a scenic display at its very doors. The literary artist was busy with circulars and handbooks for the East and South, and for the professional traveler and hunter from England, whose vacations up to that time had been spent in shooting the wild beasts of Asia and Africa. Every scheme to advertise the promising future of Kansas City was used by the city council and the citizens. Mr. C. C. Spaulding, a young newspaperman and civil engineer, in December, 1857, published a book of about 150 pages showing the natural advantages of Kansas City and giving a short history of the town and the enterprise of its merchants. Copies were handed the passengers on steamboats as they landed at the wharf. The boats gave ample time for the passengers to view the city, and when sightseeing was over a sumptuous banquet was spread in the hotel on the levee front. All this kindness and hospitality had its results. Some of the passersby made investments in real estate before leaving, others afterwards, and all remembered and told others of their favorable impressions of the city. The stir at the wharf, the large amounts of incoming and outgoing freight, the oxen trains on the levee loading and unloading, all presaged a coming metropolis. The commercial standing of Kansas City became a subject discussed from the source of the Missouri down to St. Louis and off to the far East. Never even in its many boom days of the '70s and '90s, did Kansas City attract such attention. Its growth looked substantial, new buildings were going up, business houses increased, and the limits of its city lines were outgrown.

CHAPTER IX.

CIVIL WAR DAYS AND THE BURIED TREASURE.

A DARK portentous cloud was soon observed in the east and south. The financial depression of 1857 was but a light visitation compared with the threatened disruption of the Union of the States. Civil war had been hinted and seemed imminent. The burning question of slavery could not be settled in the legislative halls at Washington. It was thought for some time that a compromise had been effected by the drawing of the Mason and Dixon line. All south of that line would continue to recognize slavery of the colored race. North of that line white and black would be free citizens. The question of admitting the Territory of Kansas into the sisterhood of states swelled the slavery issue into a heated discussion and soon into threats of disunion and war. A new political party came into existence and made its first appeal for extinction of slavery in the presidential campaign of 1856. It was defeated at the polls. Its candidate was General Fremont. It was the Abolition Party. Defeat only aroused a determination to force its principle by war measures. The new state was to be the field of contention, no matter what the nature of that contention. Young and determined "Free Statesmen" came in numbers from Boston, Brooklyn and the New England States, and bought lands and went into the cities of Kansas along the Missouri River and built up towns in the interior of the Territory. They published newspapers and made speeches in the little settlements, demanding that slavery be kept out of the coming state.

Strange to say, many of the most ardent advocates of making Kansas a Free State were people living in Kansas but natives of Southern states. They wanted no slaves in the free atmosphere of their new home. Missouri was for slavery and its spread. Each side brought forward its most violent if not its ablest orators. Threats followed intemperate speeches. Violence and bloodshed with armed invasions into Missouri and back again into Kansas were frequent. John Brown was driven from the West. He renewed his efforts of forcibly wiping out slavery in the State of Virginia. He was captured by the militia of Virginia and was hanged.

The election of Abraham Lincoln in 1860 was soon followed by civil war. The whole nation was paralyzed for four years. Missouri was the seat of war during all those terrible years. St. Louis was under martial law and so was Kansas City.

Jackson County from the admission of Kanzas Territory into the Union of States, and all during the Civil War, was a storm center for Unionists and Secessionists. General Ewing's "Order No. 11" devastated nearly all the county from Independence south, east and west. Many of the inhabitants were ordered south of the Mason and Dixon line, and many fought with the North and the South in the armies. The county was almost depopulated, and Kansas City and Independence fell off in population. The sale of army supplies was the only business transacted.

The Battle of Westport was waged from October 21st to 23rd, 1864. This made Kansas City a battlefield. The citizens were divided on the issues of the day, and were fighting under Generals Price and Curtis during those three days. Father Donnelly's parishioners and friends were on both sides. He was personally acquainted with the commanders. The first sound of the clash of arms found him on the battlefield to give his priestly services wherever needed. He helped as nurse to bandage the wounds and stanch the blood of the fallen and helped to carry the stricken to places of security. He heard confessions and prepared the wounded for death, and whispered consolation to the dying; he removed the dead, and in the darkness of the night dug trenches in which to bury them. When Price retreated southward he directed the removal of the wounded to improvised hospitals in the deserted buildings in Westport and Kansas City. For several long weeks he gave every moment of his time except while saying Mass to this work of charity. All business had ceased and Kansas City seemed deserted except for the work of physicians and undertakers. Father Donnelly had been a leader in the days of Kansas City's progress; now in the night of its affliction he was its consolation and its closest friend. People looked to him as to a father. When angry contention was inflaming men's passions to war no man could say he took side either way. Whatever were his sentiments he hid them in the secrets of his soul. He voted at every election, but never attended any political meetings during that time. He saw that war was inevitable. His constant prayer was that this land of freedom and happiness would survive the shock of bloody conflict and emerge a stronger nation and a more brotherly family. His services at the Battle of Westport were thanked in the military orders of the two commanding generals.

On the eve of the Battle of Westport in the fall of '64 panic was in the air. Sterling Price of the Confederate Army had won a victory over the Union troops under Mulligan at Lexington in September, 1861, and now rumors of his approach

to attack Kansas City and Westport flew thick and
fast.   Before leaving Lexington, it was learned,
Price had seized on the funds in the local banks
and the fear was widespread that he would do the
same thing when he reached Kansas City.   There
was a rush on the banks, accounts were checked
out by hundreds of people and the money taken to
their homes and concealed in various places.   Then
the thought occurred to many of them that perhaps
their homes would be looted, and they began to
look about for more secure hiding places.   At that
time Father Donnelly was Kansas City's "Vicar
of Wakefield," known and trusted by everybody,
Catholics and Protestants alike.   He was known
to be an old acquaintance of many of the Confederate leaders, and a friend of General Price, personally known and respected by his soldiers as well.
It was known that previous to his coming to Missouri, his life, after leaving Ireland, had been spent
largely near the Mason and Dixon line.   He had
been an Irish patriot in the homeland, and that
meant a rebel.   So the belief grew that Father
Donnelly would be one man that would be immune
from search by the invading army and the one
man who could be trusted to conceal securely the
threatened funds.   The afternoon before the Battle
of Westport hundreds of his own countrymen and
church members, as well as a large number of
others, came singly and in twos and threes up
through the trees and ravine adjoining the pastor's
residence and church, bringing money in cans and
jars and purses, and asking Father Donnelly to
take care of it for them until the trouble was over.
They felt certain that Price would not molest him.
They knew that his ministrations as priest would
be in demand for the dying and the wounded of
both armies and that his person and his property

would be held sacred by even the worst of the marauders.

He often told that he had shrunk at first from the great responsibility thrust upon him as caretaker of other people's money in those troublous times, that he tried to convince the people that war was no respecter of persons when army needs were pressing, and that a contingency might arise in which he would be no more immune than the rest of them. But they would not listen to him. The women wept and the men pleaded, and he finally yielded to their wishes. They came like so many depositors to a bank. He opened up a memorandum book. He entered names and amounts. The darkness of the evening was growing. His only light was from one small candle which threw a fitful glimmer around the room. He had been a schoolmaster before he became a priest and the methodical habits of his teaching days clung to him. He wrote out carefully and stopped frequently to read over the names, to see if he had spelled them right. The waiting crowd grew nervous and restless. Price was at the edge of town, he might be at their doors in a few hours. Many of the women, anxious to get back to their homes and little ones, threw their pocketbooks on the table, simply saying: "Here, Father Donnelly, there are so many dollars there. You know our names and where we live. Put it away for us. We must get back home."

When the crowd had finally departed, Father Donnelly said, there were bundles of money left there without any name attached and impossible of identification by memory of the words or faces of those who left them. The reader may judge what an unbusinesslike jumble it all was for both priest and people. But they were in the midst of the

panic and terror of war and heads were not cool.
It was a choice of saving or losing all, they thought.

When left to himself, Father Donnelly was
shocked by his foolhardiness.   A thousand misgiv-
ings went through his mind.   How would he get
the money out of harm's way?   Where would he
find a secure hiding place?   Then the thought came
to him: "Dead men rest untouched in the graveyard; I will bury the people's money in the cemetery."   The cemetery was two blocks west of his
residence on Broadway.   It ran along Pennsylvania
Avenue from Twelfth to Eleventh Streets on the
east, and west about 150 feet from what is now
the west line of Jefferson Street.   The gravedigger
lived nearby.   Carrying the money in a large
wooden box, Father Donnelly went in the black
night to the sexton's home, called him and told him
to get a wheelbarrow, a spade, and a broom.   Together they entered the graveyard and soon found
a plot of grass growing in a pathway.   The sod was
carefully removed and a hole dug in which the box
was buried.   Then the sod was replaced and the
loose dirt carefully swept away.

That very night word came to Father Donnelly
that Tom, the old sexton, under the influence of a
few drinks, had divulged the secret to a crowd in
a saloon at Main and Eighth Streets.   After a
hurried consultation, four trusty men, armed with
shotguns and led by Father Donnelly, went to the
cemetery, dug up the treasure and buried it anew
back of the little brick church.   After the guard
retired the priest began worrying about the security of his new hiding place, and before daylight
went out alone, with no prying eyes and no one to
be burdened with the temptation of his confidence,
dug up the box a second time and gave it another
burial in a remote spot some distance north of its
second hiding place, pacing the distance between

them and marking down, as he thought, the accurate measurements and landmarks of the new depository.

The Battle of Westport came on. The three days that the battle was waged from the Kansas State line through Westport toward what is now Swope Park were busy days for Father Donnelly. His good offices as priest and nurse were in constant demand. The dead and dying filled the homes all along the countryside adjacent to the battleground. When Price retired south the priest returned to continue his Samaritan work in the improvised hospitals of the city. It was fully a month before he was able to resume his duties in the church. When he was able to return to his own house his first thought was of the buried treasure. It seemed best to him to transfer the box to his house and call upon the owners to come and get their money. Taking a spade he went out under cover of night and dug in the spot where he was sure the box had been hidden.

An hour's labor brought nothing to light. With anxious forebodings he went back and measured the paces he had counted from the angle of the church and dug again; moved a few feet further and dug again; then a few feet northward—but there was no box. Daylight found him still fruitlessly digging. The next night was a repetition of the previous one, followed by the startling conviction that he had hidden too well or someone had spied too keenly. The box was never found.

Father Donnelly, when he had abandoned all hope of recovering the buried money, went to a friendly banker, made an estimate of the sums that had been placed in his hands, and borrowed the money necessary to repay them, giving a mortgage on some farm lands as security. As the claims were presented he paid them off.

Ten years afterwards Father Donnelly was stricken with fever. There was no hospital here then and no professional nurses. He was cared for by his aged sister and two nieces in his home, and the good Sisters of St. Teresa's Academy lent their aid. One night he seemed much improved and his relatives and the Sisters felt that he could pass the night without attendants. He had told them so and begged them to go to their homes. Early the next morning the Sisters went to his door, found it open, and the patient gone. An alarm was spread and after some time spent in anxious search the venerable priest was found, in sparse attire, digging in the graveyard. In his delirium he had fancied that the lost treasure had been moved back to its first hiding place.

Again a few years, and Father Donnelly was himself carried to the cemetery and like the wooden box in his enforced trust, some time later he was taken up and buried in another grave in the basement of the then new cathedral, where, "After life's fitful fever he sleeps well." To the last days of his life the buried treasure was on his mind. Its disappearance was a mystery that has never been explained. Whether in the excitement of the times he had forgotten the real hiding place, or whether someone else discovered it and removed the box during his absence, was never known. If it still remained in the earth perhaps by this time it has moldered into dust, or perhaps some digger's spadeful of earth will yet reveal the secret.

CHAPTER X.

RECONSTRUCTION DAYS.

KANSAS CITY seemed for a while to have lost its very life. Many of its citizens were wounded, dying, or dead, or still fighting in the closing days of the war. Peace brought home the soldiers of the North and the South. Angry feelings soon subsided. An old ambition was revived, an old rivalry was aroused, the cry of peaceful days was taken up and went from mouth to mouth: "Let us make Kansas City a great city!" Meetings were called. The object was Kansas City's good. Father Donnelly could be seen at every meeting. He joined in the discussions and cordially seconded every good scheme. Kansas City's population of from six to eight thousands before the war was down now in the hundreds. The rival cities all had suffered from the war, but none so much as Kansas City. War had entered Kansas City's gates—the other cities only felt its shock. Every city on the north turn of the Missouri River was striving for the same result—supremacy on its banks. Kansas City held that position before war days. She had been the Gate of Entry. Supremacy now would belong to the first city bringing an eastern railroad into its limits and then forcing that railroad over the river to the mountains and to the Pacific Ocean. Railroads were becoming the means of travel and the way of transportation—quick transit for man and freight. Steamboats were slow in comparison. Kansas City business men—there were no capitalists then nearer than St. Louis, New York or Boston—had lost their savings of years of industry; the few men who had valuable property

had lost it or could hardly be called owners because of mortgages and taxes. St. Joseph still held
its solid citizens. Atchison was ambitious for as-
cendency and was backed by aspiring, eastern-
spirited people in Kansas. Leavenworth was the
trading post for the army and wealth increased
there during the war because of the government's
fort and its patronage. Weston was a steady town
secured by its judicious, saving German citizens.
"A bridge across the river," was the slogan. Meetings were held in all these towns and after much
enthusiasm adjourned to create further sentiment
and to reach the approval and help of everyone in
the respective neighborhoods. Kansas City was
just breathing—resuscitation had hardly taken
place. Eastern newspapers were joking about the
fight of the Missouri River towns to build a bridge.
Kansas City's name was never mentioned among
the rivals.

On winter nights in 1867, Father Donnelly used
to relate, a few old chums would frequently meet
in the back room of the little rented Postoffice
near the river, to laugh and joke over the contest
for the bridge in other cities, doing their usual
guessing and well wishing. As the pleasantries
subsided one of those present cried out: "What
about Kansas City's getting into the fight?" A
guffaw laugh followed. Then an interchange of
hospitality. Then the question was renewed. The
fun in the question gradually abated. Kansas
City's contempt for its northern neighbors and
rivals seemed to grow in the little gathering. No
arguments followed. Kansas City in the past when
it meant anything never thought of discussion—
it simply saw and did the thing. "We can get all
the money needed; we are not poor. Our banks
will back up their customers. Let us get going."
Checks were drawn out. Everyone present was

a committee to arouse the bankers. Horses were mounted and every man with money within a radius of ten miles was ordered out of bed. When the second morning cast its light, reports were nearly all handed in at the rendezvous. The bankers accepted the checks and drew up orders on their eastern correspondents. The amount demanded to insure the bridge was on hand. Before noon four of Kansas City's enterprising citizens had started for the nearest railroad, miles east. When they presented themselves in the general office of the railroad interests away off in Boston they handed their certified checks from Kansas City banks to the capitalists who owned the North Missouri Railroad, now the Wabash Railroad. Those checks were large enough to justify bringing the railroad from Cameron Junction to what is now North Kansas City, then Harlem, and to meet the bonus for the bridge. On July 4th, 1869, the completion of the bridge was celebrated. St. Louis sent two dozen cars crowded with its best citizens, headed by the mayor and common council. The best of feeling was exhibited by the rival river cities in the hundreds of people present from St. Joseph, Weston, Atchison and Leavenworth. Kansas City's supremacy was admitted and Kansas City's hospitality was in keeping with its conquering greatness.

Father Donnelly spent days on horseback soliciting additional subscriptions for the bridge among his old neighbors in Jackson County. On the day of the celebration he figured on the various committees. War was over, its rancour had dissipated, Kansas City was established as a fixture. No man was happier than the patriotic priest.

Colonel Van Horn, owner and editor of the Kansas City Journal and one of Kansas City's best and most loyal citizens, is authority for the statement that Kansas City had fallen in population from 6000 to less than 1000 in 1865. The United States census of 1870 showed it a city of 32,000. Its growth went on.

The failure of Jay Cook in 1873 brought on a commercial collapse that passed from Boston and New York to San Francisco. Kansas City scarcely felt the shock. Three of its strongest local banks failed in 1874 and 1875. Grasshoppers swept the state of Kansas, its tributary and mainstay, of every blade of grass and every vestige of corn, wheat, oats and vegetables in 1874. A dishonesty in the city's finances amounting to some hundreds of thousands of dollars forced an issue of script that was accepted outside the city at less than twenty cents on the dollar. Inside of one year it was everywhere accepted at its face value. Three wild real estate booms brought their natural result. Yet Kansas City grew and its population in 1880 was more than fifty thousand.

CHAPTER XI.

FATHER DONNELLY A MISSIONARY.

FATHER DONNELLY was resident pastor of Independence from 1845 to 1857. His headquarters and his home were there. His assignment was not confined to the little village of the Kaw—Kaw Town, or the town of Kanzas. He was instructed to traverse at least once a year all that part of southwest Missouri from Kansas on the west to the lines of the Lexington parish on the east, and south to the Arkansas state line. As the reader stops in amazement at the little world Father Donnelly was to traverse, it should not be overlooked that this is the same Father Donnelly who a few days before he came to this expansive charge made his first trial at horseback riding on his way from St. Louis to Old Mines. The reverend Father was not an enthusiastic youth full of dreams of sure victory and impossible defeat. "There lies my mission," sprang to his mind, but the poetic temperament, if ever his, was not his to make conclusion with "and I'll make it a garden of ease and pleasure." The new pastor had bade farewell to more than forty years of a struggling life. When he painted a dream picture he went to the realistic style. Here was a field of labor covering over 20,000 square miles. The examples of early missionaries in the Illinois country, along the lakes and in the far Northwest, and along the Missouri River and south into Texas, were indeed encouraging. "If those could do such deeds why cannot I?" The real red-blooded Irishman never takes a dare and when the seasons favorable for traveling came Father Donnelly was on his Indian pony. He had mastered

the horse as he had mastered many an awkward and
stubborn difficulty.   Three different times in his
twelve years at Independence he went southeast
and west wherever he knew there was a Catholic
and where he thought he could add to the Church by
a conversion.   He touched every excuse of a town
in his demense—there was not a single hamlet big
enough to be called a town, by the people, much
less to be entitled to the name by a legislative requirement.   A number of the Catholics he found
here and there were cold in faith as in practice.
Others had intermarried with non-Catholics and had
joined some of the sects.   He preached and said
Mass in school houses, very few and far between,
then, in Missouri.   On more than one occasion he
spoke to the "natives"—a popular name and a
cherished one—in their little rude churches when
their own religious services were over for the Sunday.   Although the times were rife with the pre-
judices and hatred against "Romanism" consequent
on the nation-wide spread of "Knownothingism,"
Father Donnelly was happy to say that he received
an attentive reception wherever he lectured.   In Independence, also, he attended the civic and even
know-nothing meetings and took part in the discussions.   The kindness he experienced made him ever
afterwards extol the American sense of fairplay.

He studied the real American character and
became convinced it compared favorably with the
best he found in the people from other countries.
They were innocent of the world's worst.   Their
lives were simple.   Existence was a struggle.   They
were illiterate because there were no schools in
the East and South where they sprang from—
there were no books.   The farms they entered were
small and scarcely productive.   Their methods of
farming were crude in the extreme.   The lethargy
of the hot South was embedded in their every fiber.

They were devoid of ambition, they could not go higher and they never dreamed of improving their condition. They seemed to have no red blood in their veins; their blood was poisoned by the miasma from swamps and upturning of hitherto untouched soil; their faces were thin and pale. They were a race of new aborigines in that they had the wandering spirit and the listlessness of the Indian. They had his readiness to resent an injury or an insult, they had his long-sightedness and quickness of vision; they could bring down the fleetest bird and would face the fiercest animal that prowled the sandy plains or rugged mountains. The passing stranger was ever welcome to their frugal meal and invited to partake of their hospitality.

The visits Father Donnelly made these people resulted in a few conversions, and he felt his time well spent as he recorded that some fallen-away Catholics and their families came back to the Faith. During his absence from Independence his kind friends and predecessors on the mission at Kansas City and Independence, the Jesuit Fathers who were in attendance along the Missouri from St. Louis, looked after his parish.

He had just made his third tour, in 1851, to the south and east missions when he remembered a long-promised visit he owed his old friend Father Hammil at Lexington. Before going to his friend's home he stopped at the village hotel to secure stable and feed for his horse. The weather was intensely cold. The cheerful fire in the hotel office invited him to take the chill out of hands and feet and body. The office was filled with men who were listening with close attention to a man who was telling about a marriage ceremony he had witnessed a few days before in a Catholic church at Independence. The richest man perhaps west of St. Louis was married by the priest of Independence to a young lady named Ann Eliza Keane, scarcely. seventeen years of age. The groom was fully eighty years old. The news was so unexpected and the event seemed so unusual that men expressed their doubts and thought the narrator was just making up as he went along "But, I tell you," the man would say, "I was there, I saw it, and I saw the old gray-headed priest of Independence performing the ceremony." Father Donnelly was the priest of Independence and he was grayheaded, but he knew there must be a mistake for he had not performed that ceremony, he had not been at Independence for nearly six weeks. He could no longer restrain himself, and in loud tones interrupted the speaker: "I am the priest of Independence and I know nothing about such an occurrence." "I don't care who you are, my dear sir, I assure you I saw it all as I have said. I know Mr. Jabez B. Smith and I am acquainted with the bride and her family " It was too much for Father Donnelly. He forgot all about his contemplated visit and went at once to the stable where he delayed just long enough to give his poor pony time to finish his oats and hay. He then turned the horse towards Independence. "Jabez Smith, my parishioner and old friend, married to that dear little child of my flock? Impossible! Not to be believed!" When late the next day he reached Independence, he did not have to inquire; people stopped in the street to tell him about the marriage. It was a surprise that made people forget all the gossip and all the news of the day. He was told that Father Murphy, the pastor of St. Joseph, Missouri, had been telegraphed for and came to perform the ceremony. The newspaper stories about the marriage were lying on his desk. "And that both parties should have kept the marriage a secret from me!" If often happens that

the hardest part of a bad story is kept for the end
of the narrative. Father Donnelly had to hear the
same finale from every narrator: "And just to
think of it, Father Donnelly, Mr. J. Smith gave
the stranger priest one hundred dollars!" "Did the
St. Joseph priest leave that money here for me?"
he inquired from his domestic. "Why, no, Father;
he showed it to everyone; it was one hundred dollars in twenty-dollar gold pieces."

Time cures many wounds, but not in this instance. The pain rankled in his breast twenty
years afterwards as he would recount the affair.
One hundred dollars seems today a trifle to worry
about. But in 1851 one hundred dollars in gold
was equal to a thousand dollars in bank notes and
in purchasing value. The money the laborer, the
mechanic and the merchant handled was known as
wild cat currency and was issued by the banks. It
was worth its face value one day and the next day
the failure of the bank that issued it made it
worthless. Every little town had a bank or two,
and the banks, to the extent of the subscribed and
sometimes paid-up stock, sent forth paper bills
frequently greater in amounts than the banks had
stock or cash or credit. The result was bank col-
lapses every little while. To protect themselves in
handling the paper currency the merchants subscribed for and had on their desks a paper called
the Director, published every week in the larger
cities and containing the names of the banks fail-
ing over the country. Father Donnelly had filed
away a number of paper bills which he had accepted during those days. On their face they
amounted to several hundred dollars; in fact, they
were valueless. Now comes an opportunity to be
enriched with $100 in real money; but he was
away from home. Another clergyman had benefited by the absence. When Father Donnelly wrote

him to return the money, the answer came, "The laborer is worthy of his hire. The distance back and forth to perform the ceremony, and many other inconveniences, were well worth the offering." "I was then a priest about six years," Father Donnelly related in after years, "and all I ever received on occasions of baptism and marriages, if all added up, would hardly total $100 in currency, much less in gold."

CHAPTER XII.

CATHOLIC BEGINNINGS AT KANSAS CITY.

THE title of Resident Pastor was given Father Donnelly on the day of his ordination when he was assigned to Independence. The title was a recognition of the advance of the church on the west boundary of the St. Louis diocese. Father Le Roux could hardly be named a resident pastor, for that would suggest a residence and a fixed class of parishioners. While at the Kaw he lived with the Chouteau family and spent some time at the Chouteau agencies in the Territory. The Catholics near the Kaw when Father Le Roux arrived were Canadians who had come from Trois Rivieres in Canada and who claimed Canada for their country and home, who came as laboring men in the employ of the American, the United States, and the Astor Trapping and Fur Companies. Numbers of them came to the Kaw. Few of them were married and even those few did not stay long. They were river wanderers. The small per cent who continued here were restless and indifferent to future development. Some bought farms in the west bottoms, but nearly all lost them in the flood of 1844. The Canadian Catholics who purchased property along the bluffs overlooking the Missouri River had Indian blood in their veins or were married to Indian women. They could not, they would not, build church, schools, or support a pastor. The Chouteaus were western Astors on a small scale. St. Louis was their business center, and their warehouses were nearby, first at Chouteau Landing, east of the site of Kansas City, then on the Levee, then in the Territory. You could trace them, for they gave their name to every post and new place they located. They were good business men and at least their wives were good practical Catholics. Their home was always open to the priest and their gratuities made life bearable for the missionaries. The writer sang the Mass and preached at the funeral of the original Mrs. Chouteau.

To the Catholic Banner Father Donnelly on March 7th, 1878, wrote the following letter:

"We are not to suppose that Kansas City when first founded could be embellished by fine specimens of superb architecture; the humble log cabin alone afforded shelter and security to its primitive inhabitants. The axe, the hammer and the augur were almost the only building implements in use. The hardy hunters, with their wives, found the Chouteau trading post a convenient market for their furs and peltry. Many of them settled down in the neighborhood and formed with their families the first Christian congregation on the site of Kansas City. About the year 1834 the Reverend Benedict Le Roux, a pious and learned French priest, was sent from St. Louis as pastor of the half-breed congregation at Kansas City. During his stay a contract was made with the late James Magee—the father of all the Magees—to build a log church and parsonage. "Parsonage" was a misnomer. It was never large enough or conveniently enough arranged to be an abode or residence, in any sense, for a priest. No one ever thought of even finding a night's lodging inside its confined walls. Why, people tell me that I lived there; they call it Father Donnelly's first parsonage. I have to hear this and sometimes read it in the papers, but I grew tired long ago denying it. It was even a poor shelter in a storm. So-called historians of the early days persist in saying the passing Jesuit missionaries, and I, in my time, lived there. Whenever

I remained here over night from my residence in Independence, and when the Jesuits were here for a stay, we always made our home with the Chouteau and Guinotte families. Father Le Roux built the lodge or resting house as well as the log church. The brick in the chimneys of both church and lodge are said to be the first ever manufactured in Kansas City."

He then mentions the names of passing church dignitaries who visited Kansas City and Independence in the early days, names which are given in another part of this volume, after which he presents to the readers of the Catholic Banner the Right Reverend Bishop Barron, at that time helping Bishop Kenrick in his large diocese. This diocese extended from the Mississippi River, taking in almost all Upper Louisiana. About the Right Reverend John Barron, Bishop of Liberia, he says: "He stayed a month between Kansas City and Independence, awaiting the arrival of Father Verreydt, S. J., on his way to the Pottawatomie Mission. Bishop Barron accompanied him to the mission and returned to Kansas City on the last day of the year 1845. On the first day of January, 1846, I came to Kansas City to see the Bishop. He asked me to take a walk. The day was fine. The Bishop spoke with enthusiasm of the Indian country, describing it as the finest land in the world. We proceeded through the woods to the edge of the bluffs west of Colonel Coates' present mansion. Whilst looking to the west he raised both hands above his head and exclaimed: 'No government on earth can much longer deter the whites from entering that Territory! It is the most beautiful country in the whole world. In ten years the government will be compelled to pass an act opening that country to white settlers. When that event takes place (turning his face to the east) you *shall have an immense city around here.'* The act opening Kansas was passed in 1856, just ten years afterwards, and now (in 1878) the immense city is actually here!

"How did it happen that Kanzas Town had such an attraction for travelers of all professions? For clergy, traders, trappers, and explorers? The answer seems to be, the facilities of travel rendered by the great rivers as far west as the mouth of the Kaw. The railroads lately constructed follow the same line, and like the rivers, they diverge in many directions, making Kansas City a natural center; and thus has the prophecy uttered by Bishop Barron thirty-three years ago been fulfilled."

The Santa Fe trade, not the influx from Canada, was the making of Kansas City. No one realized this so quickly as Bishop Kenrick. His first visit to the church at the Kaw found no priest awaiting him. Likely it was not the Sunday for the ministrations here of the Jesuit missionaries in the Territory. The Bishop advertised his presence, baptized some babies and older children in the log church, leaving the names of those baptized to be "entered in the church registers at Westport." There was no church at Westport and there were no registers kept there. The paper on which the bishop wrote the names of the newly baptized looks like the flyleaf torn from an account book. It is interesting to know that this leaf is at St. Mary's Mission, and the entries made in the only register of those days, the one kept by the Jesuit Fathers. There never was a church at Westport until Father Donnelly in 1866, out of his own pocket, purchased from Mr. Jowel Bernard a site with an old-fashioned southern home. The Annual Church Directory published by Lucas at Philadelphia was placing churches in the St. Louis diocese that Bishop Kenrick was unable to locate in this first trip to the Kaw or indeed ever afterwards.

In two of the published letters of Father Le Roux there is strong evidence that the good Father could dream of what was coming. But a Jesuit Father while at the Kaw dreamt of what was really taking place. He tells of the daily and Sunday services, how the people attended, how they gladly formed themselves into sodalities and confraternities, how they became choir members and strung out in processions, how confessions and communions grew weekly in numbers. Where did these people come from to justify or make possible sodalities and confraternities? The zeal of this good Father was beyond bounds and so were his dreams. If the piety he described ever existed here it was never witnessed by any other priest, and must have disappeared with the priest who recorded it. But "memory" is a very peculiar thing. Father Ponziglione, a Jesuit Father at Osage Mission, wrote in the early nineties (1893) that he recalled a stately church at Westport in which he frequently said Mass. It must have been a fairy church, for it vanished away, leaving no marks upon the real estate records at the county seat, and no recollections in the memory of such persons as Mr. and Mrs. Dillon, or the early settlers of Westport surviving in the nineties. Mrs. Dillon was the first white girl born in the vicinity of Westport. Besides, if Lucas Brothers' Church Directory is trustworthy in its date, Father Ponziglione was in Cincinnati in the year 1849. He came to the Territory in 1851. Father Donnelly, who was here for six years previous and rode to Westport now and then, often mentioned the graphic description of how piety flourished under the short administration of the passing missionary above referred to.   "The Reverend Father," he said, "was gifted in many ways: he was very pious and rather inclined to dreams.   I never found any traces of his mission services here, and for his civil engineering and map drawing, his imagination and not the scene before him, nor his training in that science, supplied the sketch."   The Jesuit Father heralded his dreams broadcast through Catholic papers in New York and Philadelphia.

A little while after Bishop Kenrick's visit, he sent Bishop Barron over the diocese to confirm and to report the needs of the Church.   It is significant that after doing what he was sent to do at Kansas City, Bishop Barron went to the Jesuits and requested them to look after Kansas City. Father Verreydt without delay renewed his work here.   The probability is the Jesuits were finding their labors at home with the Pottawatomie tribes and the Indians at Kickapoo too taxing for their periodical visits to Kansas City.

CHAPTER XIII.

LETTERS TO THE CATHOLIC BANNER—
FIRST MISSIONARY VENTURES.

EDITOR Catholic Banner: I promised you in a communication of April last to give your readers a map of the missions attached to Independence in my letter of appointment. Your request naturally comes from a desire to know just what was the territory I had to cover. It is interesting to your readers and to all young priests to be informed what was demanded of a priest in 1845.

The Bishop's letter of appointment read as follows: "You are hereby appointed resident pastor of Independence, Missouri. From Independence you will at close intervals say Mass and hear confessions at Kaw-town on the Missouri River near the Kaw River. All Jackson County and every county immediately south of Jackson and east of the Territory to the north line of Arkansas, will be your southwest limit; then eastward; your northern line of labor will embrace Henry County and every county south of Henry to the north line of Arkansas. While you are on this missionary tour be sure to write the Jesuit Fathers in charge of the Pottawatomie Indians to say Mass and hear confessions and attend sick calls in Jackson County." Instead, I secured the services of priest from the St. Louis College, who frequently came up as far as Lexington.

I give you the boundary lines within which I was to labor. Since I am a civil engineer and map maker I could send you a map as you requested, but reproducing a map on newspaper pages is neither an easy nor a good looking job. My first trip south and east to the north line of Arkansas was started immediately after Pentecost, 1847. I left Independence with a very thorough map of the country I was entering drawn up by a competent surveyor and engineer in the U. S. service named Louis T. Craddock. He was a friend and neighbor who lived near me in Independence. His present was a map of large proportions, most complete in details, with rivers, streams and elevations, and marked with the easiest roads for travel. As he had on more than one occasion traveled in his official character through my missions and had formed many acquaintances, he knew hotel and tavern and hospitable farmers through the territory. He was a Catholic and made it a point to reach Catholics and encourage them in their seldom-attended country.

The greatest difficulties of this first entrance into my mission land were removed by the kindness of my friend. My compass stood me in good service. My observing neighbors had frequently told me that my horsemanship had improved wonderfully. The Jesuit Fathers who never tired giving me practical suggestions for missionary life advised me shortly after my arrival here to buy an Indian pony. It was sure-footed, not easily frightened by snake or wild beast, could climb like a goat, and endure heat and storm and long fasting like a camel. Besides and best of all the Indian pony was native to the soil. He seemed to know everyone and everything on the journey— like the Indian he never noticed anything or anybody provided he was let alone. His speed was an easy lope, but for a little while at a time he would hasten his pace. He never grew lame and never showed fatigue. In my knapsacks, hanging from the back of the pony and down his sides, I had three heavy Indian blankets, a few pounds of coffee, some sugar and hard army crackers, my breviaries, chasuble, with all other requirements for Mass and altar. I found room for a water-proof coat and two changes of underwear. I started out under a clear sky and found a comfortable bed that night. The second day began propitiously, but about noon a storm broke over me. The rain lasted all day and night. In the darkness I missed my bearings and soon discovered I was off the road. Fortunately I had wandered towards a stone formation and was out of the mud. With the light made by my flint and steel I saw a large stone ledge fully two feet high and under the circumstances ideal for a bed. I covered my pony with one of the blankets and the other two I used for a soft cover over the large rock and for warmth and protection from the rain. I slept well and was up and on my journey early in the morning. I soon found my trail and before nine o'clock came up to a stream of clear water fringed on both sides by trees. Here I prepared my coffee and ate my first missionary breakfast. During the next few hours I caught up with two men well acquainted with the country and many of its people. We were in Cass County. My traveling companions were from Kentucky but were then living in Missouri and were dealers in real estate, we call it now—it was then just buying and selling farms. They kindly directed me to a Catholic family living about where Harrisonville is. The family were all Catholic, born in Ireland, and had been two years "drifting," as they said, from New Orleans to their present home. They were on a small farm and living in a comfortable farmhouse. They had two neighbors a few miles south who were Catholics, too. They begged me to stay with them until they could bring their neighbors, and then would I be good enough to say Mass and give them the benefits of the Sacraments. I surely would. I was favorably disappointed in finding Catholics so soon. Mass was said and the Sacraments approached. The terrors of the long journey ahead of me began to leave me.

My host and his Catholic neighbors had wandered considerably coming here and had hunted far south of their homes in search of birds for their tables. Fresh meat was out of the question. Why, even in Independence, it was pork dried, pork salted, week in and week out. A farmer would notify us that he was about to kill and butcher a heifer or cow, and how many pounds and what parts of the carcass would we buy? Fresh meat was purchased by the hotels at the levee from steamboats, but after seven or eight days of river travel the meat needed the immediate care of ice, and ice formed here in winter, then melted. During my part of a two days' stay I feasted on prairie chicken and delicious birds peculiar to the country. My three Catholic friends insisted on accompanying me through Bates and Vernon counties where they were not only companions and guides, but where they brought me to three Catholic families and succeeded in locating four more, making in all ten families, and with their own three families thirteen altogether. I performed the Divine Services twice in Bates and twice in Vernon counties. After the return of my friends to their homes the sunlight seemed to depart. I was not lonesome, for I was a student of nature. I would dismount from my pony to examine loess as I saw it change from stone composition to a black, productive soil. I had studied rock, I carried with me the geologist's hammer. The trees were interesting in themselves. They were of hard bark and were in some instances

called iron—an appropriate name, for the presence
of such trees told of iron, lead and other valuable
deposits.   I had no Catholics to engage my mind
and time, so the Earth, and especially this part of
it, occupied me.

In Vernon County (near Nevada of today) in
following my friend Mr. Craddock's directions, I
found an Irishman named Donnelly.   His wife was
not a Catholic but had been taking instructions in
the Catechism.   She was instructed and well disposed, and so for the first time in my mission trip
I administered the sacrament of baptism.   On the
expectation of finding more Catholics nearby I remained under the hospitable roof of my namesake
for three days.   He and I scoured the country
around and brought back with us a German Catholic named Latmer and a Kentuckian named Hawkes.
Their families were all Catnolics and were at
Mass on my third day's stay.   A John Fagan
added one more to our audience.   As fortune had
it there was a public meeting in a large square or
clearing near a Protestant church to which everybody was invited.   This church was a typical
country church of olden times and faced the country road.   The preacher and myself met the first
day I was there and became friendly.   He told me
of the coming meeting and invited me to be present
and to say something.   I promised to do so.   The
object of the meeting was to work up a site for a
coming town.   The attendance filled the church.
Two of the prominent speakers failed to attend.
The preacher and myself were the only orators on
hand.   "There must be four speakers," said the
preacher.   "You'll talk two times and I'll talk two
times.   You see we must give the people all we
promised."   When three speeches were delivered
all was said that could be said regarding the ad-
visability of starting a town and how to go about

it. So when it came my second turn I told them that a real true speciman of a Roman priest stood before them. "Look for the horns, you won't discover any hoof. You'll see in me a real out and out American citizen. Now," I said, "you find the Catholic priest human like yourselves, and I'll pass on to tell you what I, a priest, and every other priest preaches." I stopped after fully three-quarters of an hour, but there was a universal and emphatic demand to "go on, go on." I did so. When I concluded the preacher said, "I wish our friend, this good priest, would give us a talk in this church tomorrow afternoon. Tell us about the Pope." The crowd voted in favor of another speech and on the Pope. I felt that some prejudice, at least, might be removed, so I gave the talk about the Pope. Those people lived scattered around for miles, but they were on hand next day. They gave me the closest attention and a vote of thanks. On my arrival at home I found a letter from the preacher who told me he had thought over my speeches, had studied the Catechism, and would like more Catholic literature. I sent him the literature. One year afterwards he called on me and entered the ranks of the church. He was baptized, for he assured me that preacher though he was he had never received the sacrament of baptism.

On my third and last trip on mission I called again to find a new clergyman in charge, who invited me to stop over on Sunday and take charge of his pulpit, as he wanted to visit friends down in Arkansas. I did so and the people saw for the first time Holy Mass and heard another Catholic sermon. This time my subject was the Mass.

My first tour followed the tier of counties from Jackson in a direct line to what is now McDonald County. I returned by the counties immediately

east.   My return was devoid of the interesting
features of the trip south.   The Catholics were
fewer and the scenery less diversified.   I found
traces here and there of the work of the Lazarist
Fathers through those parts.   At four places they
spent some days preaching to the natives.   A distant relative of the Hayden family at the Barrens
told me that the Fathers were anything but encouraged by their efforts in the counties they
visited.   I heard eight confessions, baptized two
infants, prepared an aged sick man for death.
This was the result of my first returning visit. The
two other missionary trips were almost devoid of
results.   I saw few Indians on my tours, and no
uncivilized ones.

But I saw a wonderful country, fertile and
rolling.   People in search of healthful and productive localities will surely come here and in numbers.   I have often heard of the wonderful scenic
beauties and grandeur of the mountain countries
along the range of the Rockies.   I doubt if there
is anything in the far west more beautiful, more
picturesque, than parts of the Ozark range through
which I drove.   The mountains of the far West are
awe-inspiring, but the Ozark range places before
you pictures unequaled for diversity.   The cascades,
the streams of clear, cool water, traverse the mountain sides and going down into the valleys give a
vitality to the soil.   I have never seen even in Ireland grass so green and in such abundance.   Like
Ireland, the Ozark country has its tales of valorous
deeds of an ancient people who fought every invading tribe.   The Spanish adventurers occupied
for years all that portion of Missouri.   They were
not there for health, nor for love of Nature's
charming scenery.   It was not the unsurpassed
fishing and hunting and trading with the Indians
that brought them and held them there.   Long

years before gold deposits were discovered and the famous Phillebert Mine was located. Silver mines were opened and operated by the Spaniards. Phillebert was one of a family who were among the earliest settlers of St. Louis. He left St. Louis to kill wild animals and birds and Indians almost immediately after his arrival. He had a business eye as well as an adventurous soul. He established a trading post near the point where the James River empties into the White River. He was adopted by the Delawares and went with them into the Ozarks. From the Indians it is supposed Phillebert learned of the mines called for him. The location of these mines was held secret from his very family. He would frequently leave home for long intervals and always returned with a large quantity of silver. His silver is classified as "horn silver."* I feel sure there is wealth in abundance in the specimens of stone I have seen. But the stone I saw in the neighborhood of some easy ascending grades (in Carthage) will prove the very finest building material. It is almost as white as the famed Carrara marble in Italy.

I have already drawn too largely on your columns and on the patience of your readers. My three missionary journeys were not prolific of much spiritual good. There was no growth of population from my first to my third visits. The Mexican War had sent people out of my southwestern territory rather than brought any increase. I met General Kearney and his troops on their way to the Rio Grande, also Colonel Donaldson, my friend, who led the Missouri regiment. It was a great pleasure to me to shake the hand of General

*Horn silver is the chloride, which when pure is 75.3 per cent silver. It occurs in hornlike masses, of a grayish color, turning black on exposure to light. It is so soft it can be cut with a knife.

Shields on his way to war. I spent a night and a day in his tent over two hundred miles south of my home at Independence. The general and a goodly number of his command approached the Sacraments during my stay with him. My third and last long southern mission ended in a financial disaster—I missed the honor and felt the loss of the donation given by Mr. Jabez Smith on the occasion of his second marriage at Independence.

Kansas City and Independence advanced in population and in importance as a consequence of the Mexican War. Today there are priests and parishes in many places not then on the map in southwest Missouri. Springfield, Rolla, Joplin and Carthage had no existence in the '40s and early '50s. Mark my prophecy, a bishop will soon rule all that country and his see will be in Kansas City. As I often said to you, there will be a bishop yet in Wyandotte. There were never any prophets in our family; they were always too busy trying to live in the present and trying to forget the past, to give a thought to what the future might bring forth. I may have some more recollections for the good Banner very soon.

BERNARD DONNELLY.

THE DRAKE CONSTITUTION.

Editor Catholic Banner:

Perhaps we old-fashioned missionaries and our pioneer flocks and neighbors did not make much history. Well, we went through some live eras of development. The state motto of Kansas covers the history of life in the new West from the twenties and thirties up to the year of Grace, 1879. How proudly and truthfully our western neighbors describe life out here· "Per Aspera ad Astra." In every new country people suffer for want of life's comforts and sometimes life's necessities. In other

districts east of the Mississippi the first settlers
and the builders of the present civilization carry
in their systems the poison of miasma common to
new countries. So do we—we grew thin and weak
and sallow from ague and swamp fever, and weak
and nervous from the overdosing of quinine, ipecac,
tincture of silver and other medicines administered
to destroy the effects of the exhalations of the
swamps and new-tossed earth.

Life is more than a venture in a newly touched
country. On the border line of Kansas and Missouri the air and the soil, the insects and the wild
beasts and the Indians might be endured, avoided
or made innocuous. The new country furnished
hardship enough. But the civilization from Boston
and south of the Mason and Dixon Line was forcing on us the curse of civil war. "Slavery must
be abolished," cried Wendell Phillips and Henry
Ward Beecher. "Slavery shall not be abolished,"
cried back Senator Haynes and Jefferson Davis
from south of the Mason and Dixon Line. "We'll
fight, and even die, for our principles," said both
North and South. And for years before the clash
of the Civil War they did fight and made battle
fields in Jackson County and the Kanzas Territory.
The four years of conflict never gave this county
a day's respite. Everywhere else the war closed
at the surrender of General Lee at Appomattox.
Not so in Missouri. Our state was a battlefield for
the four years of carnage between North and South.
The soldiers from both sides returned to Missouri
when the Union troops were reviewed by President
Johnson and his cabinet at Washington and when
the army of Jefferson Davis was disbanded. Peace
came back with the veterans of four years. But
it was the peace which meant that the roaring of
cannon had ceased and that drilled men were not
marching against each other in battle array. The

rancour that brought on the war had not died out. The boys of the blue and the gray were working on their farms and at their avocations again, but the marplot was busy. Perhaps he had not fought in the war days. The Southern cause had been beaten to defeat and surrender. The screws of revenge had to be tightened. The political statesmen who had lost neither life nor limb, but who had grown rich and fallen in love with power of office, saw a scheme for holding on to what he had acquired and adding to it. Missouri needed a new constitution. Judge Drake and many other good haters knew just how to draft a constitution that would give play to their ambition and the power to humble their beaten ex-Confederate neighbors by depriving them of the right of franchise. The old know-nothing bigotry would have a chance to injure a church, known as Catholic, but in their vocabulary "Romish." They soon drew up a new constitution and handed it to the voters for adoption. There was little time wasted in formulating into the document all the cunning, hatred and injustice necessary for their purpose. Some of the most vicious and vindictive of the designers and drafters of the new constitution crushing out freedom of thought even in the right of franchise, were foreigners barely able to speak and understand our language, men who rose up against Fatherland in order to gain for themselves what they were now denying native Americans who allowed them to live when defeat drove them from home.

An exasperating scrutiny and the refusal in thousands of instances to accept votes against the adoption, besides a public disfranchisement of loyal native citizens, made an easy victory for the new constitution. It was called the Drake Constitution for the man who inspired it. All professional men were barred their calling if they refused to take

an oath of loyalty. Ministers of the Gospel could
not preach until they subscribed to the oath. A
citizen who had at any time even thought favorably of the dead cause of the South was disfran-
chised.

Archbishop Kenrick ordered a protest against
the oath and a refusal to take it. Every priest
said his archbishop spoke for him. Many clergy
men of protestant sects refused. The Catholic
priest receives his authority to preach from the
Divine Master through his Orders.

Only three or four priests in Missouri were
arrested. Father John Cummings, the young pastor of Louisiana, was arrested and put in jail. It
is believed the arrest was made by a blundering
deputy counsellor in the office of the United States
Attorney, Patterson Dyer, who was absent in the
interests of the Government. He was in St. Joseph,
Missouri, pleading a case. There was no man in
Missouri more pained by this arrest than Mr. Patterson. He never so much as thought of making
his dear friend and fellow citizen of Louisiana a
victim of the Drake Constitution. He telegraphed
an order to release Father Cummings and hastened
home on the first train to undo the outrage. But
Father Cummings refused to leave his cell. Archbishop Kenrick ordered Father Keiley of St. Louis
to go to Louisiana and say to Father Cummings it
was his wish to leave the jail, which he did. This
arrest was the death-knell of the Drake Oath
His Grace employed the best legal talent of Missouri, headed by Alexander J. P. Garasche, to test
the constitutionality of this clause. A hearing was
brought before the Missouri State Court. The state
court of course sustained the validity of the arrest.
An appeal was taken to the Supreme Court at
Washington, where the decision of the Missouri
court was reversed and the oath declared unconsti-

tutional. This decision met with universal approval
all over the nation. The Radicals (as the party in
power in Missouri was called) were chagrined,
yet many of the more conservative among them
were loud in approval. Not only lawyers, doctors
and clergy were victims of this oath, but school
teachers and professors in colleges as well. The
entire faculty in the Seminary at Cape Girardeau
and the Sisters of Loretto in charge of the female
academy there were arrested and forced to appear
at Jackson, the county seat, where they were detained for several days at the convenience of the
judge. The interference of the governor of the
state quashed all proceedings in this instance.

All legal expense towards nullifying the Drake
Oath in both lower and higher courts was borne by
Archbishop Kenrick. That mild, retiring and inof-
fensive clergyman belonged to a family which had
in its day a coat of arms bearing the device, "Noli
me tangere," in English "Don't touch me."

England, France, Germany, Italy and ancient
nations have time and again tried by law strategy
to interfere with the right of the Church to preach
the Gospel of Christ, but like Drake and his Missouri Constitution have been foiled. Its laws are
God-given and its rights have the seal of Heaven
on them.

CONCERNING ARCHBISHOP KENRICK.

Editor Catholic Banner:
This correspondence will be devoted to Archbishop Kenrick. While teaching school in Philadelphia I called on the Very Reverend P. R. Kenrick, then professor of Theology and Rector of the
diocesan Seminary. He was a brother of the Right
Reverend Francis Patrick Kenrick, bishop of Philadelphia. He was several years younger than his
brother. Young as he was (he was hardly thirty

years of age) he had the measured, steady gait of today. He looked fully five feet, ten inches, tall, was not spare but athletic in build, and a lover of long walks. After the afternoon classes he left the seminary for this daily exercise. Punctual in everything, he opened the front door to the second at 4:30 p. m. He always walked alone. Weather made no break in his daily routine. I heard from one of the professors that he owed his health to daily walks. It seems he was very delicate the last year in the college of Maynooth, and after his ordination he was appointed chaplain to a convent outside of Dublin. It was thought by his Metropolitan, Archbishop Murray, that parish work was too severe for him. He had ample time for his chosen exercise and soon grew rugged. He was invited to the Philadelphia diocese almost as soon as his brother became bishop. He was immediately assigned to a professorship in the seminary and in a little while became rector. He was also Vicar General. For some months he was pastor of Pittsburgh, then recalled to the seminary. He resigned this position and was to go to Rome to become a Jesuit. His traveling companion was Bishop Rosatti of St. Louis. The bishop took a fancy to the young man and petitioned Pope Gregory XVI to appoint him his coadjutor in St. Louis. This was done without consulting Father Kenrick. When he called on the Pope what was his surprise to learn that he was to be coadjutor at St. Louis and take charge of the diocese during the absence of Bishop Rosatti, who was made Apostolic Delegate to a South American country. The Pope informed Father Kenrick that he wished him to accept the dignity. He and Bishop Rosatti soon returned to America, where on November 30th, 1842, in the cathedral of Philadelphia, he was consecrated Bishop by the Right Reverend Joseph Rosatti.

Bishop England preached at the consecration.   By a singular coincidence a St. Louis priest named Lafavre was consecrated in the same cathedral a day or two before for Detroit.   Bishop Lafavre for some years attended all northeastern Missouri and Illinois along the Mississippi River.   Bishop Kenrick left for his western home a few days after his consecration.   He traveled through Pennsylvania as far as Pittsburgh.   He took a boat on the Ohio River.   He had to change steamers at Cincinnati. A delay of two days in Cincinnati detained him in Bishop Purcell's residence, where I did myself the honor of calling on him.   I was then teaching school at Lancaster.   He said he remembered my call on him in Philadelphia.

Although it was in my mind to apply for a place in the Barrens Seminary, I did not do so for Bishop Purcell was present and I had spoken to him some time before in regard to my vocation to the priesthood.   He encouraged me and talked as if he wished to adopt me into the Cincinnati diocese.   I did not repeat my call on the new bishop and did not see him again until he received me into the St. Louis diocese.   I preferred St. Louis because I wished to work among the Indians.   There were few, if any, Indians left in Ohio, and I knew that the extensive diocese of St. Louis had many tribes, some of them under the care of the Jesuit Fathers.   I was at the Barrens Seminary for some time and then transferred to the diocesan seminary at St. Louis, under the learned Father Panquin, a Lazarist Father.   Father Panquin was a man of solid piety and as a theologian and general scholar was known from St. Louis to the Atlantic.

I was ordained in St. Louis Cathedral in 1845. My theological course was not very long, but was thorough, thanks to my able professor.   Bishop Kenrick did not put aside his theological professor-

ship when he became head of a diocese, for he
visited his seminary two and sometimes three times
a week. He listened attentively to the learned dis-
courses of Father Panquin and wound up the hour
with questions and puzzles. Before the ordination
of our class the bishop spent two full days putting
us through a thorough sifting on philosophy and
theology as well as other branches of study. His
Latin was Ciceronian and he confined his queries
to that tongue. Father Panquin frequently lauded
the bishop's classical Latin.

Since the Seminary days I have not had the
pleasure and benefit of Archbishop Kenrick's company as often as I would wish. But I know him
well by his goodness and his standing in the episcopacy of America. He is first among the fore-
most. What I have to say of my archbishop is in
accord with what every priest in his diocese says
and knows. He is not only a scholar of the highest
rank in priestly lore, but he is a scientist of acknowledged standing. His translation from the
French of a learned work on Science and the Bible,
and his frequent contributions to scientific journals are acknowledged evidences that he is a
scientist. "A priest should have a knowledge of
French and German," he used to tell the students. "Our tongue has a wide range, but the
great questions engaging the thinking minds of
our day are only slightly touched by English authors. In Germany and France you find a classi-
fication of minds. They have the poets, the historians, the students of statecraft, and the supere-
minent philosophers and theologians. The reading
public patronizes them and they are not forced to
struggle for an existence. In society and the
financial world men are proud to refer to their
acquaintance with the two great European languages. The priest is by every requirement a stu-

dent.   He should be in close association with the
leaders of thought.   Remember the German and
French writers are tireless and thorough.   They
do not put together epitomes—they write exhaus-
tive dissertations."   This advice was as regular as
his visits to the seminarians.   His library is large
and select.

In appearance our Archbishop has a natural
dignity that attracts attention.   A brilliant young
priest named John Ireland, now Bishop of St. Paul,
in a series of articles appearing in a Chicago newspaper under the title of "Men and Things I saw
and heard at the Vatican Council," says of Archbishop Kenrick: "While a chaplain in the army
during the Civil War I was the bearer of some
military orders that had to be handed to a commanding officer with headquarters at St. Louis.
While in that city I visited Archbishop Kenrick.   I
had often heard of His Grace, but now for the
first time I saw him.   He was my Metropolitan,
but I was a young priest in St. Paul and from my
ordination was very busy as assistant in our Cathedral.   He impressed me very highly.   The next
time I met him was in Rome during the Vatican
Council.   I was still a priest.   I called on His
Grace at his lodgings and asked if I might occasionally escort him when he took his daily walk
on the Appian Way.   With a cheerful smile he
said, "Yes, I shall be delighted.   This walk is my
only exercise here.   There will be no Session of
the Council tomorrow afternoon.   Let us meet at
three o'clock in the afternoon."   I had heard of
his methodical habits as to time and I was at the
starting place to the second—so was His Grace.
When we reached the famed promenade, we found
a large number of ecclesiastics from minutantis
or attachees of the Vatican to Bishops, Archbishops and Cardinals.   We had scarcely joined

the array when Cardinal D'Angelis, the presiding member of the Vatican Council, approached. His eyes fell on Archbishop Kenrick and he left his companion and moved to the Archbishop, whom he shook by the hand and addressed in friendly terms, as if they were old friends. This was a happy surprise to me and I am sure to the others who saw the exchange of greetings and who recognized the participants. The Archbishop introduced me to the Cardinal. The Cardinal was the leader of the Infallibilists and His Grace of St. Louis led the Inopportunists, and had up to that moment on two ocassions mounted the tribune in the Council Chamber to reply to the arguments of the great majority demanding the Decree of Papal Infallibility. When the Archbishop and I resumed our walk, His Grace immediately took up the description he had been giving of Rome when he first saw it in the early summer of 1842. The meeting of the Cardinal and himself evidently did not weigh on my Metropolitan, but it did on me. During the two hours' walk we discussed many subjects, but not Papal Infallibility. After this first walk as well as after the others, acquaintances would say to me, "Who was the distinguished looking dignitary with whom you were walking?" Others saw charm of manner, dignity of bearing, and an intellectual face just as I had."

His dignity was natural—it was as much a part of himself as his great intellect, as his genial and even disposition. In his study he met his priests with outstretched hand and a "God bless you" from his lips and heart. The St. Louis clergy invariably fall on their knees as they approach and after a blessing kiss his ring. His first and usual question follows, "How is your health?" Then, "Take great care of your health, for it is the greatest asset a priest has." Then a momentary silence.

or a reference to the weather. The priest broaches his business. The archbishop counsels or recommends, or if he sees so, advises adversely. More good wishes follow and the priest asks another blessing, confident that His Grace has advised wisely. Gossip, politics, tales about priests or the diocese are never entered into by the archbishop, and should the priest offer such subjects the expression on the archbishop's face and a forbidding look would mean that the interview was over. No reprimand in words. A witticism in the natural trend of the conversation would be graciously acknowledged and followed by some amusing remark by His Grace. He enjoys a pun and shows approval at any witty scintillation by a smile or quiet laugh. His modulated tones are easily heard. Loud language or high-toned singing are grating to his ear. His singing on the Altar is sweet and correct with the notes of the rubrics. When visiting a priest for confirmation, cornerstone laying, or church blessing, he strives to save all unnecessary attention and begs to be allowed to feel at home and to put up with the ordinary everyday run of things. His visits always leave happy recollections. He never departs without thanking the domestics for their kindness.

He must be slow to chide, for I on one occasion seemed an offender. When an act of direct disregard of obedience was telegraphed the Missouri Republican, I know he read the printed falsehood and quietly awaited my statement. The misrepresentation referred to was consequent to the order of the Archbishop for every priest to read to his congregation on a certain Sunday a condemnation, and a refusal to obey the Drake Constitution commanding ministers of the Gospel to take an oath of allegiance to the state government of Missouri and not dare preach until the oath was

taken and signed.   This order was a claim that
the right to preach the Gospel came from the state.
The pagan enactment of old was resurrected.   I
read the archbishop's letter and entered my protest in clear, strong terms.   My closing words were:
"When the united sentiment of condemnation of
the state's claims and the state's interference with
our God-given authority and commission to preach
the Gospel reaches the capital at Jefferson City
the bigots will weaken and deny they meant what
they enjoined.   The papers tell us that one of the
originators of this anti-Christian demand is already
weakening and said, "If they persist in refusing to
obey, we may compromise and allow the preachers
and priests to lecture on the Bible."   In one of
our pews sat a disreputable man who a few days
before was arrested by our Mayor during a sword
practice for a duel with one of our citizens.   Besides being a wild-eyed, quarrelsome man, he spoke
on frequent occasions shockingly disrespectful
things about religion.   He claimed he had been a
Catholic, but long since left the Church.   In the
Catholic Church at Jefferson City he interrupted
the priest in the pulpit and broke out into a blas-
phemous harangue against the Pope, bishops and
priests.   His guiding evil spirit led him to my
church this morning.   He surely saw in the newspapers that the archbishop's letter would be read
and the new law defied.   He had now and then
dabbled in newspaper work.   Here was a chance
to lie against a priest and an opportunity to earn
a few dollars as correspondent.   The story he sent
the St. Louis paper was that Father Donnelly said
he would obey the constitution and instead of
preaching would for the future lecture on the Gospel.   All he telegraphed filled a column on the
front page of the St. Louis Republican.   I had
heard tne archbishop say he rarely read more than

the headlines in a paper.   The interesting story
about me likely led him to read from beginning to
end.   I only surmise, for I never heard him refer
to the matter.   But several of my clerical friends
became solicitous about me and sent me telegrams
of doubt, denunciation, and fear as to my certain
fate.   The St. Louis dailies did not reach here then
until late in the afternoon.   I hastened to purchase
the Republican of that morning and when I read
it I sent a telegram to my archbishop vigorously
denying the statements and regretting that I was
an innocent occasion of grief and chagrin to him.
I also sent a long message by wire to the Republican, which it published on Tuesday morning.   I
soon learned who the correspondent was and lost
not a moment in trying to meet him.   But, coward
and liar that he was, he left the city early Monday
for parts unknown.

My second untoward venture had a business
intent.   It was backed by a desire to save the archbishop from the bungling of an inexperienced man
in whom his Grace had confidence.   For several
years he was in the employ of the archbishop as
his superintendent in the construction of the many
buildings the archbishop was erecting on vacant
diocesan property.   It was in 1869 and His Grace
was preparing to attend the Vatican Council in
Rome.   He made it known that during his absence
this builder would represent him as his business
agent and would have charge of the sale of many
tracts of land in the new parts of the city.   The
Celini estate left by a Father Celini to be disposed
of after a certain time and the proceeds used for
the benefit of keeping old and decrepit priests of
the archdiocese of St. Louis, was to be put on the
market.   Here was a matter that concerned the
priesthood of all Missouri—their property was in
the hands of this lay agent.   Like Shakespeare's

Caesar he had grown great, and his meat was the archbishop's patronage.   At a called meeting in the rectory of a St. Louis priest, diocesan clergy from city and country missions drew up a mild and reverential protest against this appointee handling as agent the bequest of the St. Louis priest to priests.   If His Grace insisted on selling this grant, there were priests in the archdiocese who could handle the sale more judiciously than he and would by their management bring better financial results. The paper was signed by all present.   The names they selected as worthy and competent agents were among the senior and experienced priests.   They were: Rev. William Wheeler, Rev. Patrick O'Brien and Rev. Bernard Donnelly.   These reverend gentlemen were a committee to hand the protest to His Grace.   That afternoon they waited on the Archbishop and read the document to him.   Each one in turn said a few words, laying stress on what they called the ignorance of this party on real estate values.   His Grace listened with utmost attention.   When we had finished a heavy silence followed.   It seemed, but really was not, long when he asked each one of us, "Are you through, Reverend Father?"   Our reply was, "Yes." Then opening the door of his study he said, "Good day, gentlemen."   The Celini estate was sold.   I learn, for I was not present, that the Vicar-General, Very Rev. P. J. Ryan, at the annual meeting of the Priests' Purgatorial Society of the Archdiocese in the Immaculate Conception Church, St. Louis, November, 1870, called on the priests present to start a mutual aid society for old and infirm priests. To the question of Father P. O'Brien, the Vicar-General replied there were no funds in the archdiocese for needy priests.   I have at my elbow a copy of the Acts and Decrees of the St. Louis Synod held in 1852.   There the fund is mentioned.   I

knew Father Celini and heard him state that he
had put aside legally a tract of land in St. Louis
for poor priests.

No wingless angels in human shape swing in-
cense around Archbishop Kenrick. A glance from
his soul-penetrating eyes would still the flatterer,
and words of reproof would paralyze the tale
bearer. No coterie of the self-seeking kind could
endure in this diocese. His selections for honors
always have been men of brains and good work.
"Take him for all in all, I shall not look upon his
like again."

During the four years of the Civil War, Archbishop Kenrick never crossed the lines of his own
diocese. When his brother, Archbishop Francis
Patrick Kenrick of Baltimore, died suddenly in
July, 1863, he did not attend the funeral. No
provincial assembly of the bishops of the Province
was held, although one was due but recalled. Provincial synods or councils were regular every few
years. His Grace carried out all the details of the
beautiful ceremonial of Holy Week. He pontifi-
cated on Holy Thursday and Good Friday, and
invariably preached on both days. Pastors and
assistants of all the city churches attended in the
Sanctuary. After the Easter of 1861 His Grace
never appeared in the Sanctuary during the period
of war except to say a low or early Mass, and to
confirm and ordain. All during the conflict of
arms he practiced prudence in word and action.
On one occasion, a student of theology belonging
to St. Louis, notified His Grace that he had been
drafted into the army, and begged advice. Archbishop Kenrick's reply was as follows:

"Dear Sir: Prudence forbids me to do more
than acknowledge the receipt of your letter.
Yours truly,
P. R. KENRICK."

Priests imperceptibly pattern themselves after their bishop. The St. Louis clergy are studious, hardworking and pious. Their reputation for these qualities is recognized the country over. It is an honor to belong to Archbishop Kenrick's diocese.

B. DONNELLY.

CHAPTER XIV

FATHER DONNELLY AND HIS BROTHER PRIESTS.

FATHER DONNELLY lived so far away from his brother priests and kept himself so busy at Independence, Kansas City, and his missions, that he seldom found time to visit them. Even in his home town he rarely called on anyone except for business purposes. His well-selected library grew dearer as he grew older. His Greek and Latin books were ever at his side. He read them, he translated them day after day. He purchased every new work on science and history. Murray's English Grammar was well thumbed and frequently brought into requisition while entertaining a visitor. His writing and correspondence were done after the supper meal was over. The light by which he wrote was a small sperm candle held in the mouth of a soda water bottle. He wrote slowly, every little while taking up the manuscript and looking at it to find if the "t" was crossed and the "i" dotted, and the word spelled correctly. Then he had a habit quite common in his day of leaving the letter or writing unfinished, to be continued the next night. As he closed his writing he would draw a line under it and put a new date on the next page. Some of his letters run over five or six days, which meant five or six dates.

The school-room and the desk had the effect of making Father Donnelly in after life at times a recluse in the sense that he rarely left his home or city. When some strenuous effort engaged him for a lengthy period, such as collecting for church, hospital, and other edifices, or some wear and tear like the Westport battle and its consequent work among the sick, wounded or dead, occupied his time and attention, he sought relief and relaxation by retiring to his little home and going forth only at the call of business or duty. His habits were well fixed before he became a priest. He enjoyed company and could indulge in joke and repartee and above all was ready in argument when discussion arose. All such pleasant opportunities had to come to him, for his visits were sudden and short. If his predecessors, the missionary Jesuits, had ever gone over his territory, they went in turns, one man this time, another the next. Strong as he was physically he needed and took occasionally a long rest. When rest and quiet were over he saw many things to do. His clerical friends were miles away. He no doubt yearned for congenial company and he knew that could be found only when priests came together. The coming together of priests strengthens them all, their example is effective, and their interchange of sentiments and experiences helpful and encouraging. The passing missionary from some monastery or religious house, and a few priests of the diocesan order were all who could afford to come to Kanzas or Independence. Father Donnelly was as little able to defray traveling expenses as they were.

The missionary waiting for passage on a northbound boat would drop in on him at Independence or Kanzas. At Independence he would share his confined quarters with his guest and in the '40s and early '50s he brought the visitor at Kanzas to the commodious and hospitable home of the Chouteau family. It should be mentioned that many of those chance guests were so inured to the hardships of their lives on the frontier that they slept by choice on the hard floor, being so unaccustomed to the luxury of a bed that it afforded them only a restless night.

During all this time Father Donnelly was at Independence, at Kanzas, or on his annual two or three months' journeying to the Ozarks. When Kansas City assumed metropolitan proportions, priests usually found quarters at the local hotels, and during their stay would rarely forget to pay their respects to the pioneer Father Donnelly. Every caller went away impressed with his adaptability. He could bandy jokes and pleasantries with the most waggish; he could sing a comic song with the visitor who would display his acquaintance with and the rendition of an Irish ballad from Moore or some well-known maker of rhymes. If the caller offered a challenge to a philosophical or theological discussion, Father Donnelly hurried to pick up the gauntlet.

Busy Father Donnelly feared to leave his home lest the call to some duty would find him absent. "A priest is a soldier of the Lord and should forever be at his post," he would say. Although slow to give account of his way or ways of doing things, or of his treatment of others, more than once in letter or by word of mouth, he would remark: "I cannot be happy with assistants because they are forever on the go; they don't try to be at home in their rooms." Father Kennedy was his closest neighbor. They had the same ideas of clerical propriety. They both more than once tried but failed to bring to task the "guerilla clerics who were ever seeking after the goods of other parishes, if not the good." Those men he was free to call "marauders who wear sanctimonious faces and shake their heads with piteous terms of disapproval of other priests' endeavors." In sickness. in death, Father Donnelly was first at the bedside of brother priests. His purse was open to the wandering and destitute clergy. Father Donnelly was a priest among priests. His high and holy calling he brought to the attention of priest and laity alike. A judge (Judge Latshaw) of high standing, who in his childhood days lived near Father Donnelly, said in a speech referring to early settlers· "I lived as boy and young man near Father Donnelly's home. I saw him several times each day, but I can never recall his going in or out of his home, or moving from the church back three blocks to the graveyard, that he did not wear on his head the three-cornered cap and his long robe or cassock. He was always a priest!" This is no small compliment, and is an evidence that the man who spoke so frequently and so highly of the priesthood was glad to display his sacred regalia. It was only to see Father Donnelly daily to know that he was first and always a priest. While his life brought others to a high appreciation of his vocation, he constantly lauded brother priests who were true to all priestly, gentlemanly and scholarly requirements.

Father Donnelly was a manly priest—he would have been as manly in any other calling. He was too big mentally and in generosity of heart to be jealous or small in the estimates he made of others. He saw men who did little in the priesthood or for the priesthood advanced to high positions. He was quick to point out why each one went up higher. He even searched for reasons for some promotions. His charity was bountiful and yet his honesty was as great as his charity, and his boldness of expression was as great as either. It was generally believed by his friends that his last years would be rewarded with some special recognition. Some admirers among the clergy petitioned his Grace in St. Louis to use his good offices with Rome to make Father Donnelly Monsignor, then, and for many years afterwards, a dignity unknown in America. His Grace replied by saying that there was no honor too high for Father Donnelly and that he would bear in mind their request. Father Donnelly learned what the priests had done and wrote them thanking each one for his kind intentions but finding fault with them for writing the letter. He also wrote a letter to Archbishop Kenrick saying that he had reached the highest honor for which he was ambitious—he was Father Donnelly and wanted to rest with that.

CHAPTER XV.

HISTORY OF THE ORIGINAL CHURCH SITE.

FATHER BENEDICT LE ROUX, the first resident pastor, purchased in 1839 forty acres from Pierre La Liberte for the sum of six dollars. He deeded ten acres of this to Bishop Rosatti for a consideration in hand of two dollars. On the ten acres, when deeded to the Bishop, were a log church and a log sitting place for a missionary priest. It was entirely too small for a residence. There were two little rooms, one designed for a kitchen, the other just big enough for a narrow couch and a chair or two. The church was dismantled when the city laid out Pennsylvania Avenue and Eleventh Street. The church was at the intersection of the two streets. The log hut was sold with other parts of the original purchase to help pay for the new Cathedral. $10,000.00 was the money paid for the lot on which the hut rested. The Cathedral cost over $100,000. The cathedral of Buffalo, one of the most beautiful churches in the United States, was completed by Bishop Timon in the '50s for $150,000. Material and labor were much lower when the Buffalo cathedral was built. To meet the cost of Kansas City's cathedral it was necessary to sell much of the ten acres.

Father Donnelly sold that portion of the plot facing west on Washington, north on Eleventh and south on Twelfth Streets half way to Broadway, to build or complete·the new St. Joseph's Home for Female Orphans. The price it brought was $11,200.00. When streets and sidewalks were run through the original ten acress there were left about three blocks, with about 120 feet over, lying west of the west line of Jefferson Street. The cathedral and some of the unsold property facing on Broadway and the portion facing on Washington, sold by Father Donnelly (of course with the consent of the archbishop), is the east extreme. Father Donnelly, about the time he resigned his church, opened and graded Jefferson Street from 11th to 12th Streets. The block west of Washington Avenue was used by the Sisters of St. Joseph and was the site of St. Teresa's Academy. From Pennsylvania Avenue on the west, to Jefferson Street, was the graveyard. When Father Donnelly opened Mount St. Mary's Cemetery burials ceased in the old place. Many of the dead were transferred to the new grounds. A number of graves remained untouched until Father Doherty, Father Donnelly's successor, had them all transferred to their new home in Mount St. Mary's.

Concerning the cemetery Father Donnelly wrote to the Catholic Banner, February 15, 1880:

"The churchyard or graveyard was southwest of the little log church, fenced in by upright pickets driven into the ground. The graves were few.

"There is reason to believe that the first Christians who died in the vicinity of Kansas City were buried at the summit angle of the bluff just east of the foot of Grand Avenue. I saw the rude crosses there in 1846.

"I find in the records of the dead the following primitive names, viz.: Edward Petelle, Mary Dripps, (Otto-nata), Virginia Philibert, Marie Belmore, L. Felix Canville, James Gre, Andre P. Roy, Lenard Benoist, Lessert, Jarboe, Farrier, and many others. Margaret Prudhomme, Henri Henri, etc.

"Gieso Chouteau, a gallant lieutenant in the United States army during the Mexican war, the Guinotte brothers, Belgians by birth; Dr. Benoist

Troost, a surgeon in the grand army of Napoleon
the Great, etc., etc. The unassuming people of
those days were the hardy, fearless pioneers of
religion and Christian civilization."

Safeguarding the original ten acres of church
property purchased by Father Le Roux was a constant care of Father Donnelly's lifetime. "When I
came here in 1845 I found the ten acres, the log
church and little cabin or resting house in the care
of Madam Margaret Gre, an Iroquois Indian
woman, with her six children. The poor woman
had been forced to abandon her hut in the West
Kanzas bottoms by the great overflow of 1844.
She was living in a hovel, half wood and half canvas. She kept the log church neat and tidy. She
did her cooking in a small apartment on the south
end of the log hut. She spoke English imperfectly,
but had a good command of French and her own
Indian dialect. She was strong and fearless and
at the approach of strangers carried a large stick
which she held hoisted in a threatening manner
until she was sure of the friendly intentions of the
invaders.

"It was in 1847 after an absence in South
Missouri from Independence my home, and Kanzas, my mission, that I luckily obtained the two-
fold information that a charter had been granted
and a company formed to lay off a town at the
river, and that the members of my Catholic congregation, headed by Dr. Benoist Troost, had held
several meetings during my absence at which it
was moved, seconded, and passed to sell the ten
acre lot for $500 and to accept from the town com-
pany the donation of six lots of sixty feet front
each, situated on the high bluff east of Broadway
where now is to be seen a brickyard. At that time
$500 was considered a high price for ten acres.
Next day Dr. Troost called upon me, showed me

the petition to Archbishop Kenrick, at the same
time pointing out the blank intended for my name.
The Doctor was too intelligent a man not to know
that the signature of the pastor was more potent
with the Archbishop than those of all the others
put together. So the doctor very politely and per-
suasively requested me to sign the petition. With
an assuring tone and a confiding look I asked the
doctor if it were not more politic and prudent to
address a few lines of my own to the Archbishop
and give him a more lucid account of matters and
things at Kansas City, and to point out to his
Grace the prospective impulse the starting of a
new city down at the river would give to religion,
etc. The doctor acquiesced. I wrote a letter to
the Archbishop stating everything, but warning
him against complying with the request of the
petition. Among other things I made the common-
sense argument to induce him to agree with me:
'It is true a company has been chartered with the
object of starting a new town, the site to be laid
off at the river, but I wish to remind your Grace
that if it ever be of much account, the city will
come over our way, for it cannot go into the river,
and therefore in a short time we may find our-
selves near enough to it. The town must come this
way.' The Archbishop answered: 'I do not wish
to divert the church lot near Kanzas from the intentions of the donor.' "

CHAPTER XVI.

THE COMING OF THE RELIGIOUS ORDERS.

FATHER DONNELLY'S entrance into Kansas City cut off his large missionary field on the south and to a great extent on the east. His limits were narrowed down, but his interest in the old territory was as keen as ever. Indeed, he translated the Greek word Episcopos to "guardian, superintendent, overseer." He was always the Episcopos or overseer, of his old original territory. Nothing done in his old field escaped his watchful attention. He was happy at the good, fruitful work of the priests to whom his domain was parcelled off. He lauded the zeal and activity of his clerical helpers, and was glad to return a visit from any of the new pastors.

The needs of the Church in Kansas City went apace with the growth of the city. He could not expect the required financial help from his people. With two or three exceptions they were all struggling to meet the family demands. He quoted the words of the magician: "There is gold in the ground, and with my wand I'll set it free." The gold in the West was hidden in the Rockies near Pike's Peak, and in California. He saw help and wealth in the very clay of the ten acres. He dug up the earth and shaped it into bricks. He kept his brickyard in service until the early '70s. He sold thousands of brick, and what he retained he used in the parish school. It was brick from his yards that built the original St. Teresa's Academy facing on Twelfth Street. With them he completed his residence, making it a two-story building. He readily found purchasers for his product. The financial results made him able

The first addition to the Catholic School, when it became St. Teresa's Academy. Built in 1867. Picture taken about 1869

to donate $3,000 to the German church of Saints Peter and Paul.   He gave out of his savings $2,000 in cash to St. Patrick's parish soon after it was started.   To the Annunciation parish he contributed $500, all he could then afford.   He never solicited for the purchase of Mount St. Mary's Cemetery, but bought the forty-four acres and paid for them from his savings outside of the brick industry.   The ten acres which he first intended for a cemetery, but because of its rocky soil found unsuited for burial purposes, he bought and paid for without any call upon the public.   This is the site of the St. Joseph's Orphan Asylum.

When the Civil War broke out Father Donnelly had the basement of a large brick school on Washington Street completed.   Further work on the building was out of the question.   But with the exception of the three days of the battle of Westport, the teacher, Miss Mary Virginia Haverty, now Mrs. S. Jarboe, never neglected her class one day.   They held school in the basement.   As the city's population fell from over six to less than one thousand, the school attendance correspondingly decreased.   With the return of peace the city gradually grew, and with it, the Catholic school. In 1866 Father Donnelly applied to the motherhouse at Carondelet for teachers.   When he received a favorable response he finished the two stories over the basement and built a large brick front to the original structure, facing it towards 12th Street.   This was the beginning of the future St. Teresa's Academy.   Mother Francis was the first superior.   With her were six other Sisters. From their very arrival there were evidences of success. In 1869 Mother De Pazzi replaced Mother Francis.   The city was growing rapidly, and the attendance at St. Teresa's Academy was satisfactory.   Local families sent their children there and

St. Teresa's Academy as erected by Father Donnelly

the towns of Kansas were represented in the attendance.   Independence, Lexington, Liberty and
Weston took advantage of the only convent boarding school near by and figured among its patrons.
Old St. Teresa's Academy has been forced from
its original site by the enroachment of commerce.
Its new location is in the most desirable part of
Kansas City.   The new buildings are unsurpassed
in architectural beauty and modern facilities by
the most modern female colleges in America.   The
Sisters of St. Joseph in academy and parochial
work have never lost their hold on the Catholics
of Kansas City and surrounding territory.   The
St. Joseph Hospital was suggested and aided
financially by Father Donnelly.   It began as a
seven-room, two-story frame building.   Like the
Academy the hospital yielded to the advance of
business, and its namesake occupies a commanding site in a resident district, central, and free
from the noise and influences detrimental to the
sick.   Its style of architecture has been copied in
various cities of the East.

The St. Joseph's Orphan Asylum still retains
its original location, on the ten acres donated by
Father Donnelly.   The Park Board of Kansas City
has secured the permanency and usefulness of the
asylum on its original site by swinging around it the
picturesque boulevard arising from Penn Valley
Park and named for one of Kansas City's greatest
citizens, Mr. Karnes, whose loyalty to Kansas City
and whose ability as a lawyer will live in the history of his beloved city.   The Sisters of St. Joseph
teach the school attached to the cathedral, and
are still on the ten acres of Father Le Roux, where
they instruct 350 pupils.   The other schools under
their care in Kansas City are: The Redemptorist
School, where they have over 500 pupils, in connection with which they teach a commercial course

and have a high school department; they have 95
pupils in the Assumption School; 450 in the school
of the Holy Rosary; 85 in the school of Our Lady
of Guadalupe (Mexican); and 70 in Sts. Peter
and Paul's.   In the St. Joseph Orphan Asylum
they teach the orphans and have recently admitted
children outside the institution.   They came here
with seven members to open Father Donnelly's
school.   Today they have 120 Sisters in Kansas
City and their pupils in the orphanage, Academy
and Parish schools number fully 2,000.

Father Donnelly assisted the Redemptorist
Fathers to buy their site of ten acres.   In 1876
he invited them to give a two weeks' mission in
his church.   The Very Reverend Father Provincial
sent Fathers Cook, Enright and Kern in response
to the request.   That mission was truly a religious
awakening and an impetus in the Catholic Church
of Kansas City.   The Immaculate Conception
Church was central, with St. Patrick's Church on
the east and the Church of the Annunciation on
the west.   The church (about 35x60 feet) was not
large enough for the demands of the parish, but
after the first Sunday the whole city became ani-
mated with the spiritual interest aroused in the
mother parish.   The crowds that flocked to the
Monday evening sermon filled the church to standing room.   Those who could not enter stood around
in large numbers, the windows were opened, and
the outside attendance outnumbered the inside.
Tuesday evening the schools on 11th and on Washington Streets were packed to the doors, while
the church proper held as many people as on the
previous night.   Every night until the close, three
missionaries preached in church and the two
schools.   Day after day from the five o'clock Mass
in the morning until late at night confessions were
heard.   Father Cook, the superior of the mission,

seeing what was confronting him, had two more
missionaries hurried from the Rock Church in St.
Louis. The number of confessions and Communions seemed to grow with each day. It was
a pleasant surprise to the local priests. They did
not know there were so many Catholics in their
city. Many men of social and financial standing,
calling themselves Catholics, whose wives and
children went to Mass and their duties, were
avowed Freemasons, Oddfellows, and Knights of
Pythias. They marched in the parades of these
societies. It would seem that some special grace
led these men to attend the mission. They tore
loose from these forbidden organizations and resumed their standing in the church. Kansas City
was booming at that time and many newcomers
lost no time in making themselves known to their
respective pastors as a result of the mission. A
spirit of indifference at least, or perhaps the example on the part of the home people had made
them believe it was the smart thing to stay away
from Mass on Sundays.

The two newer parishes were beneficiaries of
the mission. The following year Father Cook, with
Fathers Rosenbauer, McLaughlin and Kern, opened
a mission in the Annunciation Parish. The Catholics from the hilltops came down to the West Kansas City bottoms, and every man and woman in
that new district attended early Masses and approached the Sacraments. The two new school
buildings took care of the overflow at the spacious
temporary church. The magnetic zeal of the Redemptorists suggested to Father Donnelly to invite
them to a permanent residence in Kansas City.
Nothing was too good for his beloved city. Its
interests were always uppermost in his heart. The
growth of the church and the salvation of his people
were deeper in his every thought and prayer than

144   LIFE *of* FATHER BERNARD DONNELLY

even the material advancement of the city. He lost
no time in opening up a correspondence with the
Very Reverend Provincial, Father Jaeckel, and
then repeated his wish in a letter to Archbishop
Kenrick of St. Louis. Father Jaeckel consulted
the Father General (Father Mauron) at Rome. A
speedy permission resulted. This was in November, 1877. The Father Provincial soon came to
Kansas City to secure a site for the future home.
Father Donnelly had in mind a desirable place.
Cook's Pasture seemed to him to be central; it was
just inside the city limits. It began at 17th and
Summit Streets, running to Broadway and south
to 24th Street. It was rolling ground, in parts
well shaded by stately oaks. There were many
acres of rich, loamy soil. The price was reasonable. The Father Provincial was much pleased
and his mind was made up to purchase.

When Father Jaeckel called on the archbishop
for approval, His Grace procured a map of Kansas
City which he had filed away. Cook's Pasture
being pointed out, His Grace thought the location
was too near the other city parishes and advised
that they would go south, near Westport. "Father
Donnelly is constantly telling me that the growth
of the city is southward. Besides, as you intend
to start your work with a school for young postu-
lants, and will in a short while establish your novitiate there, I think you will find a much more convenient location on the high land near Westport.
Cook's Pasture will soon be a downtown neighborhood." The Provincial shortly afterwards returned
to Kansas City. Father Donnelly then offered him
a present of his ten acres near 31st and Jefferson
Streets. While grateful for such a generous ten-
der, the Father Provincial wished to be on a main
street or avenue running from Kansas City to
Westport. The Jefferson Street property was out

of the way. In addition, it was high and uneven,
and had a heavy rock deposit which would entail
expense in building. With many tnanks he declined
Father Donnelly's gift of property. Father Donnelly was not disheartened. He admitted that a
better site lay not many yards away. It was level
and on tne very street running south to Westport.
He would contribute to the purchase of the more
desirable property. The Mastin Brothers, then the
leading Kansas City banners, owned a large farm
south and east of Kansas City. A corner covering
ten acres facing north and extending southward
along the Westport road was for sale, the first
partition of the farm, and its most desirable part.
The deed of purchase was drawn up and signed
before tne Provincial returned to St. Louis. 'ims
property was just what Father Jaeckel wanteu.
It was conveniently located, without hill or quarry,
about two miles from Kansas City, and not very
far from the old town of Westport. The price
was five thousand dollars for ten acres.

How proud Father Donnelly was when he
learned from the Father Provincial a few days
afterwards that it was the intention of the con
gregation to use the property for the home of their
missionary Fathers and for a novitiate and college
and seminary for their students and novices. "What
an honor to Kansas City!" he would exclaim. "One
of the best known and most efficient religious organizations in the Church coming to Kansas City
to supply missions and missionaries to the whole
country from New Orleans to Detroit and from
St. Louis to the Pacific Ocean! Kansas City is
at last on the Map of Religion in the United States.
This was something I hardly dared dream of in
sleeping or wakeful moments."

The date of the purchase was December 3rd,
1877. A two-story building with a high stone base-

ment was started in early spring. The cornerstone of the structure was laid by Father Donnelly on the first Sunday of March. Reverend Father Cook, C. S. S. R., preached. Fathers Dunn, Dalton, Curran (the assistant at Immaculate Conception Church), John Ryan (assistant at Annunciation), two Benedictine Fathers from Atchison, three Redemptorist Fathers from St. Louis, and Father T. Fitzgerald of Independence, Missouri, took part in the ceremony. A large concourse of Catholics from the three parishes of the city and from neighboring towns in Kansas was present. The day was unusually fine and the sun shone as on a day in May.

The structure was finished and on May 28th, 1878, was solemnly blessed by the Father Provincial, assisted by the two resident priests, Fathers Faivre and Luette. Father Faivre was Superior. A lay brother was the third member of the community. Improvements on the grounds and the construction of an annex made the new home for the novices and students of the Province. The transfer of the novices and students from the original home at Chatawa, Mississippi, to Kansas City took place in January, 1879. Father Firley, the Master of Novices, escorted the young men to their new residence. He held this same position for many years and was local Rector in Kansas City and afterwards Provincial of the Congregation.

The Redemptorist Fathers opened their spacious community Chapel to the few Catholics south of the city limits. The little mission at Westport was practically closed from January, 1875, and in time became succursal to St. Patrick's Parish. Then it was put under the charge of the Redemptorists. Sick calls were attended by the Redemptorists as far south and east as Hickman Mills and the River Blue. This was done at the request of the pastor

of St. Patrick's Church, whose growing parish made
it impracticable to go so far away from his home.

A new duty came to the Redemptorists early
in 1880. In January of that year Father Donnelly
opened the Orphan Asylum on what is now Jefferson and 31st Streets. He handed over to them
the chaplaincy of the new St. Joseph's Orphanage.

In March, 1881, the Redemptorists were requested to attend once a month the missions at
Norborne, Parkville and Liberty. Father Beil was
assigned to these new charges. In 1882 the new
convent of the Sisters of the Poor was added to
the charge of the Redemptorists. On February
21st, 1888, the Redemptorist Parish was established.

Many of these original novices at Kansas City
have since held high positions in their congregation. At least three of them have been Fathers
Provincial, and the Rectors at St. Louis, New Orleans and other places in their western Province
made their novitiate in the Kansas City home.
The House of Students was in time transferred to
Kansas City. Newer and larger buildings followed
as a necessity. The courses immediately preparatory to the priesthood were for years taught here
and the number of priests ordained in the Kansas
City house is very large. Almost from the very
start the Fathers residing at Kansas City went
forth on the work of mission-giving. Frequently
they have given missions on the Pacific Coast, from
San Francisco to San Diego on the south, and to
Portland, and northward into the British possessions in Canada, eastward through Salt Lake, Denver, and the towns in the Rocky Mountains. In
every diocese west and south of Kansas City their
missions are recorded in the work they have done
for God and humanity. Like St. Paul they travel
everywhere and preach everywhere. Time and

Exterior and interior of Redemptorist Church

again St. Paul and New Orleans have been spiritually benefited by the Redemptorist Fathers from the Kansas City house. The churches of St. Louis, Chicago, Indianapolis, Memphis and Alabama are the beneficiaries of the zeal and efficiency of St. Alphonsus' Rectorate at Kansas City.

Father Donnelly's zeal for the salvation of souls is far-reaching in the work of his chosen Redemptorists, who gave preparatory training to their subjects at Kansas City. Their efficiency has won recognition wherever they have labored. Their novitiate is now at De Soto, their house for preparatory training is in St. Louis County, and the seminary for the closing studies before entering the Sanctuary is on one of the picturesque lakes of Wisconsin. The changes that time and opportunity demanded have consigned the Kansas City home of St. Alphonsus to mission and parish duties. The Fathers here are as ever in requisition for missions, everywhere far and near. Their parish work is efficiency itself. Their church structure is the largest in the city. When material and labor knew no such prices as they command today, St. Alphonsus' Church cost over $200,000. Their schools number over 500 pupils, and are academic as well as preparatory. New and larger structures will soon follow the pressing demands. The Church attendance packs the spacious aisles and fills the pews Sunday after Sunday. The number of confessions heard is very large. In 1920 the number of communions exceeded 220,000.

CHAPTER XVII.

FATHER DONNELLY AS A LABORING MAN.

WHEN Father Donnelly began his brickmaking, after the bricks were molded and carried out to dry, night after night he watched the moon and the sky, and when heavy clouds portended a coming rain, would not wait to call the yard laborers from their slumbers, but in his barrow and on boards would carry the bricks to a sheltered place. When the rain ceased he helped carry them back to the sun's rays. In his brickyard he wore the overalls of the laborer. He laughed heartily when passersby or strangers would mistake him for a workman. He was pleased to hear it bandied about that he was one of the hired men in the church brickyard. The church property on the east side and from the south to the west limits, was graded down to the street level by converting the elevated parts into brick. He called this result good business and the saving of hundreds of dollars. The extreme west end of the church property to the north was what he called the Rocky Point. Large bulging tiers of rock went up fifteen feet high. Between times and when his work in the brickyards was easing up, he turned to what he called the "Rocky Point." The small and the softer stones he sold to contractors who were riprapping the Missouri River. Some of the stone would make good lime. He built kilns just as he had seen them abroad. Yard after yard of stone crumbled and fell in flakes or chunks under his eyes. He called this employment "working at my old trade." Father Donnelly had the habit of his countrymen of always portraying the things at home as better than the same in America, "but my

lime was never excelled at home or abroad," was a
daily boast. He ought to know. In this, as in anything else he prided himself on, it was wise never
to contradict him, "for though defeated, he would
argue still." Builders and contractors said his lime
and brick were of a very high grade.

When he had disposed of the top ledges of the
quarry he came to a hard white vein of good building stone. He found a ready market for this to be
used in facings and steps. Here he proved himself
a competent stone cutter. Oftentimes he could be
seen by the side of the mechanic with chisel and
mallet cutting down and facing large slabs of this
native stone. Men working by his side many a time
allowed their curiosity and astonishment to get the
upper hand and would say, "Where did you learn
this trade?" His reply was the Irishman's; it did
not afford any information. He would respond,
"Sure, I had to work for my living when I was
young and hardy like yourselves." Day after day
Father Donnelly hammered and chiseled alongside
the well-known contractors, Bishop and Hughes,
who passed most favorably on his skill and used to
say they could not surpass him. The stone tracings
in the circular front window of St. Benedict's
Church at Atchison were done on stone from Father
Donnelly's quarries and with his help.

CHAPTER XVIII.

MORE LETTERS.

December, 1879.

Dear Father Dalton, Editor Western Banner:

YOUR repeated invitations to contribute to the columns of your paper are gratefully received and I now comply. As you have suggested for my topic something historical of the early days of my missionary life I will tell your readers some of the few things I can now recall. I was the third duly appointed resident pastor of Kanzas—it was simply Kanzas—no "City" affix when I came to Independence. Let me name the two resident pastors previous to my appointment. The first was Rev. Father Le Roux, who purchased the church site. Father Saulnier was the next resident pastor. He remained here only one year. I was pastor at Independence when he left here. Archbishop Kenrick wrote me to take back Kanzas as one of my missions. In 1857 Father Denis Kennedy was made resident pastor and a few days after coming here exchanged with me for Independence. From that time I was really pastor here. It was indeed at my suggestion that his Grace raised Kanzas once again to a parish. While in charge here I built the Immaculate Conception Church, facing on what is now Broadway, midway between Eleventh and Twelfth Streets. The little log church was erected by Father Le Roux. It was a log structure 15x32 feet with two windows on each side, and an entrance facing east. It rested on a stone foundation. The style of architecture, if it might be so dignified, was identically like the style of the orig-

inal churches at St. Louis, Missouri, and the ones
at Lexington, Liberty and St. Joseph. They were
really chapels and had no patron saints for many
years. Like the others, it was too small for anything resembling a steeple on top, and when I arrived it did not even have a cross above the entrance.
I placed a small wooden cross on it. Outside, on
the east side about six or eight feet away and about
two feet back from the line of the front of the
church, was a roughly-shaped belfry built of heavy
supports or beams, nearly a foot in diameter. It
was sixteen feet in height; rough pine boards made
a roof to screen the bell from the weather and I
suppose to keep the sound of the bell from an up-
ward tendency, for its warning notes were intended
to be towards the earth where they would reach
the ears of the people. Resting on the roof of
the belfry was a large cross, out of all proportion
with church and belfry. The bell was a gift from
the first pastor, Father Le Roux, after he left here
and while he was pastor of Cahokia or some little
French settlement opposite St. Louis. This bell I
gave to the Sisters of St. Teresa's Convent. It is
still used to call the Sisters to their various duties.
It also serves the purpose of arousing me from my
slumbers at five o'clock every morning. The sound
and shape of the bell resemble the steamboat bells
on the boats plying the Missouri and Mississippi
Rivers.

The walls and flat ceiling of the log church
were plastered with a rough finish. Besides the
Stations of the Cross, there was back of the altar
a painting in oil of Christ Crucified. On the outside of the small Sanctuary hung two oil paintings,
one of some Saint Bishop, standing, with mitre on
and holding a crozier. On the right-hand side of
the bishop was a true picture of his own mitred
head resting on a platter, this head being the

bishop's head decapitated. The whole effect was that the good bishop was in a trance and saw where his head was soon to be. The picture was of the Spanish school of art and looked as if it had been cut out of a large painting. It was loaned the church by the Chouteau family. The other picture on the opposite side of the altar was of a martyr being flagellated. The altar piece, Christ on the Cross, and the picture of the martyr, were surely of the realistic school, which was in striking contrast to the art displayed on the canvas of the bishop with the head on and off. The history of these pictures was that they were brought here from Mexico by some of the traders who traversed plains and mountains back and forth from Mexico. They were either purchased or seized from some of the missions in Mexico, or were quietly taken away and found a home in Kansas City.

Two rows of unpainted pews lined either side of the one aisle of the church. A few kneelers were to be found here and there in front of pews. Some boards nailed together with a latticed opening in the center, was the confessional. On week days Father Saulnier used the church for a school. He was the teacher. Among other branches, he taught French and English. My school at Independence antedated the one at Kansas City a few months. I had to help me a Miss Mullins, a member of one of our best Catholic families.

The first historic notice of the log church is made in the deed of transfer given by Father Le Roux to Bishop Rosatti of St. Louis. In the deed is the mention of a small two-room log house. I often found this hut a convenient place to sit in during my stay in going and coming from Independence. I usually read my office in the west room. Other missionary priests would while away a few hours resting in the east room. The west room was comfortable in a rain or in cold weather, for it had a fireplace and a few kitchen conveniences. The rooms were too small to be a living place. It was never Father Le Roux's intention to make it a residence. I and all the other priests attending here stayed over night and sometimes for days in the hospitable dwelling of Mr. and Mrs. Chouteau, with the Jarboe family, or at the Guinotte home. Father Le Roux lived with the Chouteaus during his stay here. It was his home; it was the home of the Jesuit missionaries from St. Mary's in the Pottawatomie country. "The priest's home in early days" is a misnomer. The hut served the purpose principally of an outside sacristy, convenient for a sitting place while the priests were waiting for confessions on Saturdays. The interstices between the logs were never properly filled. In fact, it was impossible to fill them, as the logs were so uneven and the knot holes so numerous. The wood was decayed. It had been part of some hovel somewhere before used here. To the missionary, accustomed to sleeping in the open, the log cabin would be a misery and would give him rheumatism.

The church and cabin and ten acres were all given and paid for by Father Le Roux out of his own funds. He had some private means when he came here and had no expensive habits. I never had the pleasure of meeting Father Le Roux, he was gone before my time. He paid a short visit to his old parishioners late in 1844—in September, after the great flood. He did little missionary work while here, contenting himself with following up some Trois Rivieres Catholics who were working at the various Chouteau agencies, or who were engaged in hunting and trapping. La Liberte, Pierre Chouteau, and those who were here in his day, lauded him for his piety and refinement of mind and manner. Father Lutz spent a few days here in the early spring of 1844. Father Saulnier, my immediate predecessor, was from Canada, where he served as pastor near Quebec. The West did not appeal to him. He was well spoken of, and my acquaintance with him made me respect him highly. He had all the enthusiasm of the French pioneer priest. He opened up new books of marriages and baptisms. Those records from the coming of Father Le Roux, some entries made by Father Lutz and some passing priests, were deposited for safety in the Chouteau warehouse on the levee. The records were swept down the swollen river with the warehouse. A few leaves with baptism entries were found afterwards in the Chouteau home and were handed me. The records made by the Jesuit Fathers were taken home with them to their mission house at St. Mary's. Fathers Ward and Stuntebeck, rectors of St. Mary's College, informed me that the records made here and taken to St. Mary's are in a good state of preservation, at their flourishing college in Pottawatomie County.

This communication is entirely too long. I don't write as easily as I used to, and the joints of my fingers do not work as smoothly as when I was young. Another letter for next week's Banner. Age has its penalties.

BERNARD DONNELLY.

December, 1879.

Dear Editor:

Let me correct my closing remark in last week's letter. I said I was old. Give me the Irishman's privilege of speaking twice, the second time to correct the first speech. I am not old. I am a Donnelly. My father died but the other day, and he was 112 years old. It was an accident that killed him or he would be living still.

But to the task you have imposed on me, per-
taining to the early days at Kansas City. I often
thought when you would ask me questions about
old times that you meant to make a history of the
information. But now you make me the writer as
you win me over to be the narrator. Who knows?
If you see it worth while you may make me a hero
of a biography.

But to the task you have laid on me: My
memory is full of the heroic sacrifices of the Jesuit
missionaries in these parts. My soul is full of
admiration of the work of God done by those good
men. They certainly imbibed the spirit of their
great founder, St. Ignatius. The greater glory of
God is their aim and their inspiration. St. Ignatius
did not court, does not take, the drone, the coward,
or the brainless. Brain, brawn, and zeal make up
the Jesuit of today. A military fire to do or die
burns within them. They know something about
everything and a great deal about many things.
I read of the Jesuits before I ever saw them. I
found them learned in the sciences and elegant in
the languages. I read of the elaborate plans and
the forty years of deep study with which they prepared to enter China and foreign countries. I
heard them tell of their brethren, and others, too,
relate of the heroism and greatness of their missionaries in China and Japan, and the world over.
But I have lived to see them with my own eyes
and I know the zeal and fearlessness of their
members in other days survive to as great extent
in the De Smet, the Eysvogels, the Verreydt, the
Galliand, of Missouri, Kansas and the Rocky
Mountains. They have been an inspiration and
an impetus to me in my territory. They have been
my friends, my advisers, and my models. I could
write for hours of what I know they did in these

parts. They have been the builders-up of religion from St. Louis along the Missouri, across the Rockies to the far-off Pacific Coast. They never lived here as residents, but their regular visits here kept religion among the Catholic pioneers fishing for a livelihood in the rivers and trapping and hunting on the plains and mountains. They never passed my poor home without visiting me and encouraging me by word and example. They cheered me when I was despondent, and they more than once used their credit and their own scanty means when I was out of pocket and hungry. This poor tribute does not do ample justice to the debt I owe them. They built up the Faith here and organized the church and made life possible for the secular priests. When Kansas City began to build up parishes, I more than once wrote the superiors in St. Louis to start a church here. They told me they could not come. The church's permanency will never be assured until the Jesuits come back to this, the scene of their early efforts. I have often prayed to live to see a church and a college here under their administration. You, the young editor, are but a boy in years—you will see your teachers of St. Louis University your colaborers here. The Jesuits, the Eysvogels, Verreydt, De Smet, etc., baptized, married and preached here. So did Verhaegen, Hoecken, Aelen, and many others of the Society.

The Lazarist Fathers, my old professors at the Barrens, hunted the stray Catholic from the Barrens to the Territory and to Texas. Father Tom Burke and another priest whose name I cannot recall, were requested by the bishop to traverse west Missouri and to report to him where he would be justified in opening up missions for diocesan priests. They left the Barrens in the year 1845 on horseback to go to the extreme southwest por-

tion of Missouri. They could find but few growing districts where a priest could live. The scattered inhabitants here and there were Protestants
from Kentucky and Tennessee. At times they
came across a Catholic who was so used to living
away from priest and church that he expressed
himself indifferent to the coming of one of his
clergymen. He feared the priest's presence would
arouse the bigotry of the neighbors. Deepwater,
one of the Jesuit missions, was a promising location. The Catholics were made up exclusively of
a German colony and they were well contented
with the services of Jesuits from St. Mary's, and
afterwards from the mission at Osage under the
supervision of Father Schoenmacher. Independence looked well and promised a future. The next
village that met their eyes was Kanzas on the Kanzas and Missouri Rivers. They returned to St.
Louis after my arrival. I was raised to the priesthood in 1845. I requested the Bishop to permit
me to visit the pastor of Old Mines for a few
days before sending me on my mission. He kindly
granted the request. That very day I started for
Old Mines. I borrowed a horse from a friend in
St. Louis and rode there. The next day after my
arrival a letter was handed me from his Grace, to
go without delay and open up a parish at Independence. I mounted my horse and returned to
St. Louis, called on the bishop (he was not made
archbishop until 1847) and with my letter of appointment I hurried to take the steamboat which
left St. Louis that afternoon at four o'clock. I
found the boat loaded with freight and over two
hundred passengers. Some of them were heading
for California, others were going anywhere west
to grow up with the country. Gamblers, who plied
their avocation on every boat heading north, south
and west from St. Louis, were on board. They

were the most prosperous-looking passengers on the boat. They could be found at the long tables on the upper cabin all day except while meals were being served. After supper they resumed their games at the tables and played late into the night and possibly early in the morning. They were flashily dressed with a great display of watch chains, and their finger rings were valuable with settings of diamonds. They were always quiet and well behaved. They evidently did not seek out their victims, for men flocked to the cleared tables without invitation. If there were any losers, and there undoubtedly were, the losers were game and kept quiet. After seven days we touched the landing at Kanzas. Although we were impeded in our progress by sand bars three different times, the trip consumed the average time.

I found Father Burke awaiting my arrival, for he knew a priest was coming. I carried a letter of introduction to Messrs. Chouteau and Jarboe, Catholic merchants on the levee. Independence was my destination. Father Burke, his companion and I procured the loan of a horse through the kindness of the two merchants and in less than three hours from my arrival were on our way to my new home. We dismounted at a livery stable and handed over our steeds to the care of the man in charge. I then faced a little hotel or boarding house where we registered. That evening I was introduced to three different Catholic families, among them Mr. Davy and his sons and their wives. Mr. Davy was a very wealthy merchant and later one of my most generous parishioners. They all looked at me as if in astonishment: A priest to reside in Independence? Why, they had been satisfactorily attended occasionally by the Jesuits. They hardly believed a pastor could get a support.

A few days, and I was nicely ensconced in a well-furnished room in the house of a newcomer to Independence, a Catholic, named Gilson, from St. Louis.

A town was growing on the river a few miles away which was a "feeder" and landing place for Independence. The people told me that a rivalry for future greatness was growing between Independence and Kanzas here and in the county.

I found less than twenty families in the town and immediately surrounding farms. But there was a vast territory from here to the end of my charge. I was told to visit at intervals from the Kaw to Arkansas. There was church property here willed to Independence by Bishop Rosatti. I finally, after many appeals, was able to purchase an abandoned carpenter shop for a church. When I had the little church ready to occupy—it was two feet longer than the church given by Father Le Roux at Kanzas—I put up a two-room cottage for myself. I used the church for a school until I could erect the one-story school house. As I could not give all my time to Independence, I hired a teacher, Miss Mullins, who was very competent.

Some years later I discovered great dissatisfaction among the Catholics at Kansas City. The church building did not suit them and the city was growing away from it. For the second time they petitioned the archbishop to sell the ten-acre lot and the church erected by Father Le Roux and put the price in a fifty-foot lot and unused building. I offered a compromise. I suggested that they rent an empty one-story frame house near what is now Cherry and Second Streets. This quieted them. We temporarily closed the log church and had services in the rented building.

When I saw my appeals meeting a response, I began the brick building on the east line of the

property facing Broadway. We had the cornerstone laid on the first Sunday of May, 1856. The
Definition and Promulgation of the Doctrine of the
Immaculate Conception gave a happy and timely
name for the new church. It was named the
Immaculate Conception Church. The name St.
Francis Regis was not given by Father Le Roux
to the log church. Father Le Roux never gave it
a patron. It was called by him and his people the
log church; that is the title given in his description when he included it in his deed to the bishop
of St. Louis. The name of St. Francis Regis was
given it by Father De Smet when the mission was
handed over to the Jesuits. Father De Smet on
his way from the far West stopped over with me
for a few days. I met him at the Kanzas City
levee. After a short visit at the home of the Chouteau family we rode up the hills to the church site.
It was while sitting in the little church cottage
that he told me about the origin of its name. He
smiled as he related that the thought occurred to
him that the chapel needed a patron and he could
not think of a better saint to watch over its destinies, so he christened it St. Francis Regis. He
said he informed the bishop of St. Louis and the
Vice-Provincial, who both said, "Now the church
is complete—it has a name and a good one."

Westport was always a concern of mine. I
knew it when it was a waiting place for the thousands going southwest to Santa Fe, and to the
mountains, and the gold fields of California, and
Pike's Peak. Like Independence, Westport was a
plateau. It was higher than the hills back of Kansas City. But I presume Nature had done too much
for Westport and left a great deal for the people
to do at Kansas City. Westport is no larger today
than it was in the '50s and '40s. The only future
I see for it is that Kansas City will throw its arms

around it in its strides southward and eastward
and annex it. It will make a beautiful residence
district for the coming giant city of the West.
The Jesuits said Mass out at Westport, as did many
priests traveling to the new diocese of Santa Fe.
Masses were usually said in tents, occasionally in
the home of Mr. Dillon. Westport was for many
years a pleasant resting place for the priests and
people awaiting Uncle Sam's arrival to take them
under his protection as they wandered through the
country of hostile enemies. It was only a few years
ago that Bishop Lamy of Santa Fe, while traveling
in a cavalcade of ox-carts and on ponies, was at-
tacked by the Indians. He had with him eight or
ten young priests, and a number of Sisters of Charity from Cincinnati, going to open up schools. The
bishop had had experience of what might happen
and made provision for the possible contingency.
He had purchased shotguns and ammunition at
Cincinnati. While he waited at Westport he practiced shooting with his young clerical friends. He
told them what would likely come. "The Indians
will like you better if you stand your ground and
shoot back. If you run away they will follow and
shoot you sure." The Indians did attack them.
The bishop formed the wagons into breastworks
and did some straight shooting, and finally sent
the Indians flying to their tents and hiding places.
One of the young Sisters died on the battlefield.
She was suffering from chronic heart disease and
dropped dead at the first volley.

There never was a chapel or church at Westport, and the two occasions I said Mass there I
officiated in the home of Mr. Dillon, a local merchant in the harness business. The Archbishop of
Santa Fe and Bishop Maschboeuf, his former Vicar-
General, now Bishop of Denver, and the priests
escorting them said Mass under tents. They made

the same use of them frequently as they journeyed home. On one occasion I visited the bishop of Santa Fe as he tarried at Westport. He had with him four elegantly attired priests who left their native France to do missionary work in New Mexico. I observed them going about in the best apparel of Paris. They wore silk stockings and costly leggings. Their coats were of rich material and their hats were high and of the latest New York style. Their rest here gave them a chance to parade in their very best. It was their last chance. Perhaps it was the shine of their hats and the richness of their attire that drove the Indians to make the murderous attack. Many a man I saw approaching the far West dressed in a metropolitan's finest, who in a little while was glad to wear the red shirt and belt and leather pantaloons.

I purchased in my own name the first piece of property in Westport intended for church purposes. I have deeded it over to the archbishop. On this property is a one-story building occupied as a residence. The parlor is used for a chapel on Sundays for saying Mass. I witnessed myself, and every priest who ever officiated there on Sunday tells me, that the little room is never filled. I am confident a church, probably churches, will dot the grown-up Westport. Kansas City has to grow; its natural and sure tendency will be to the south. Kansas City will make a ward or many wards out of Westport.

Father Halpin was an ex-Jesuit who left the Society and was appointed my assistant. He took the lay of the land and soon went to St. Louis and came back pastor of a new parish on the east of Main Street—St. Patrick's. Father Archer succeeded him, and then came Father Dunn. The first site of the new St. Patrick's was sold and a new and more desirable one selected. I had the honor of laying the cornerstone on the new site. I laid the cornerstone of the new church and monastery of the Redemptorists, out near Westport, also the cornerstone of the new and spacious orphan asylum. The Annunciation Parish was started by its present young pastor on the first Sunday of July, 1872. A hospital on Seventh and Prospect has just been opened. A large graveyard is bought and paid for and has been in use for nearly two years. People say it is too far out. The time will come when they will say Mount St. Mary's Cemetery is too far inside the limits, that it should be closed and another one procured. I will not live to see it. Kansas City in church and civic prospects has a wonderful future.

My fingers are getting stiff from writing and I am becoming garrulous, even if I am playing historian.

Yours Anon,
B. DONNELLY.

THIRD LETTER OF FATHER DONNELLY.

Rev. Editor:

It may be of interest to your readers and helpful to the future historian of the Church in and around Kansas City to give the names of the priests who have officiated at Westport. Father Gross, the first pastor of Sts. Peter and Paul's Church, attended Westport every second Sunday. He did so at the order of the archbishop. In fact he made his home out there for a few weeks but did his Sunday work at Kansas City, saying Mass here for his people and giving them opportunity to receive the Sacraments. Father Muehlsiepen, the Vicar General for the Germans in the St. Louis archiepiscopal see, did not approve of his living at Westport and came here and induced him to return to Kansas City. Father Halpin's assistant at St. Patrick's then said Mass at Westport for a few months, when Father Michael Walsh of St. Louis was appointed resident pastor. He remained in charge for six months. He organized the congregation and had excavations for a church 50x120 feet when he was called back to St. Louis to assist my old friend, Father Henry of St. Lawrence O'Toole's parish. The successor to Father Walsh was Father James Douherty, who for some little time had been assistant to Father Hennessy at St. Joseph. On the consecration of the latter as Bishop Hennessy of Dubuque, he became pastor. When St. Joseph was made a see Father Douherty acted as rector for a few months. He soon requested that he be allowed to return to the archdiocese. It was then he came to Westport. He started out by reducing the size of the contemplated church at Westport. While living here he accepted my hospitality. By assiduous efforts he raised considerable money collecting along the Fort Scott Railroad among the men working on its construction. He finished the walls and roof of the church. On the tenth of January, 1872, he was made pastor of the Annunciation Church in St. Louis. He reported a debt on the Westport Church of $3,500.00—another weight placed on my shoulders. I had bought and paid for the Westport Church property myself and now the creditors looked to me to pay this debt. As the archbishop refused to send another pastor there I felt this new obligation was mine and assumed it. After repeated letters to St. Louis I was told that the young pastor of the Annunciation Church in the West Bottoms would be given an assistant who would at least say Mass every Sunday at Westport. By way of digression let me say that the Annunciation pastor, our editor of the Banner, was living on Liberty Street in a room 8x10. He divided

up with his assistant, and had at least the comfort
of youth and health and pluck.   His assistant was
Father Michael McKin, many years his senior and
partly broken in health.   We three formed a combination and went soliciting along the railroads
and among some of the well to do people of Kansas City.   In a little while we had the debt down
to $2,500.00.   I then paid off that sum, leaving
me little of my savings.   After Father McKin left
here to become the first pastor of Joplin, another
assistant alternated with his rector, Father Dalton,
in visiting Westport.   When in 1874 Father Dalton gave up the Westport charge, it was handed
over to Father Dunn at St. Patrick's.   His assistant,
Father Cooney, was regular in his work there.
Once more and for the last time it was decided
Westport was too far to work in, and its connection with Kansas City ceased.   All this time, the
new church was untenanted.   Father Douherty
left it without doors, windows or floors, so Mass
was always said in the long-drawn-out one-story
frame building.   I repeat, Westport will yet be
heard from.   The Redemptorist Fathers are not
far away.   They have opened up their convenient
chapel for Westport and the surrounding territory.
When the Redemptorists came here it was with the
understanding that their time and their buildings
would be solely for the education and training of
young men for their congregation.   Their grounds
are large and afford health and recreation for
their evergrowing number of young students and
professors.   The advance of civic progress will in
a while demand a more secluded site for the novitiate and house of studies and their work will be the
labor of a great parish.

       For thirty-five years I have found good diges-
tion and plenty to do inside the lines of home and
parochial duty.   My farthest trip in all this time

was to journey to Quincy to the Monastery of the
Franciscan Fathers where there was a reunion of
my classmates at the Barrens, and when the few
of us left celebrated our Silver Jubilee.   Just three
responded to the call—every one of the others
had gone to his last home.   I reached Quincy about
eight o'clock in the morning and saying farewell
to my two old comrades I left for Kansas City at
seven o'clock that same evening.   I attended two
annual retreats.   I was present at the consecration
of Father Ryan as Bishop Co-adjutor to Archbishop Kenrick.   Three times I was present at the
retreats of the priests of the St. Louis diocese in
the house of my old professors, the Lazarist
Fathers, in the Church of St. Vincent de Paul.
During those early years I did not hug the comforts of my little cabins here and at Independence.
Three times on horseback I traversed the almost
solitary country from Jackson County to the
Arkansas line.   I did not find many Catholics on
those trips, and they, as a body, seemed to have
grown cold in the Faith.   I have learned that
Kansas City will soon be the home of a bishop.   A
passing bishop going home from St. Louis where
the bishops of the Province had gathered to lay
out a new diocese showed me the map of the new
see.   Except for Father Hammil's parish and
Sedalia and the mission on the eastern side of the
contemplated diocese, my mission covers the area
of the future bishop and his priests.

After three complete circuits of my missionary
field I grew serious and began to feel that if life
is worth living a man ought to take care of his
health, that long journeys with very indifferent
results, if any, and days and nights of exposure to
the weather and sleeping on the highways with
my saddle for a pillow were not good for men of
my increasing years.   The gentle pastor of Deep-

water, and the good-natured Father Hammil, and Father Walsh of Jefferson City, kindly relieved me of any more such endurances. I had plenty to do at Kansas City and Independence.

Although a poor visitor myself I had the extreme pleasure of entertaining many persons. The great Senator Benton did me the honor of a call while in Independence. Governor Gilpin who invited the Senator to Jackson County and who listened to his predictions of Kansas City's certain greatness, was my neighbor in Independence. He was a man of culture, well read in the Latin and Greek classics. He spoke French fluently and had traveled abroad extensively. He lived in the West and loved its plains and mountains. He predicted that the Territory of Kanzas which fed thousands and thousands of buffaloes and other wild animals would yet feed and make rich thousands of farmers and commercial men. He climbed the mountains of Colorado before the gold mines of Pike's Peak were opened up, and he wrote of the healing balmy climate of that country, advertising it everywhere. He afterwards held a position of honor under the government in that mountain land before it became a state. No man before or since predicted so lavishly of Kansas City. Many an evening and late in the night he visited me in my humble home and I returned his calls. His well stocked library was at my disposal and from its shelves I conned much useful lore and renewed my acquaintance with many loved authors. General Harney, when the quiet of peace would permit it, would turn his face to his St. Louis home, always dropping in to see me and tell me about the Indians, and keep me posted on the politics of Washington, and the country at large. He was a man of commanding figure, over six feet four inches tall. He was the ranking officer in the army close

to General Scott.   He knew the Civil War was coming and regretted it very much   I last saw him
after President Lincoln ordered him to St. Louis.
      Senator Lane of Kansas was my friend, as was
General Curtis, and good General "Pap" Price.   I
learned much about the war when it was in progress from those men.   I was on the battlefield of
Westport during three days of conflict.   They allowed me all the privileges of the scene of carnage.   I was the chaplain on both sides, with written permission to visit their wounded and help
bury their dead.   I found hospitals in Westport,
Independence and Kansas City for the wounded in
the homes of the kindly people of those little
towns.   Archbishop Kenrick visited me when he
came for confirmation.   Once too, when he called
on Father Meurs at Glasgow, and when he dedicated the new Cathedral at Leavenworth.   Bishop
Barron paid me the courtesy of a two days' visit
on his way to St. Mary's mission, and once when
he confirmed in the old log church.   He was a very
learned man, a priest of Philadelphia, and succeeded Peter Richard Kenrick as rector and professor of theology in the seminary at Philadelphia.
He was consecrated Bishop of Liberia.   His sojourn
there impaired his health, and he returned to the
United States on his resignation.   He aided Bishop
Francis P. Kenrick in his laborious work in Pennsylvania.   He then came to St. Louis where he did
the work of an assistant bishop, doing all the visita-
tions and confirmations outside that city.   He paid
visits to the Jesuit missions at Kickapoo, near
Leavenworth, to St. Mary's, and southeast Kansas.
He died of yellow fever while helping Bishop Gart-
land in the South.   One of my dearest friends and
visitors was James Duggan, afterwards Bishop of
Chicago, and previous to that coadjutor bishop of
St. Louis.   For a few years before his ordination

as a priest he spent his vacations with me. He would bring his gun with him and day after day would traverse the neighboring hills and plains in search of fowl. He was a trained shot and kept my larder filled with the result of his markmanship. He was a handsome, intelligent young man. His trips West were a recreation that the physicians of St. Louis prescribed for him. Although athletic in walking, running and jumping, there was a latent infirmity that afterwards made him an invalid.

Many a day I walked to the steamboat landing to shake the hands of Captain Chouteau and Captain La Barge. Bishop Miege, S. J., the first resident Bishop in Kansas, was a typical Indian missionary, a man of letters, with a gentle, kindly heart. He resigned his high honors to go back to his Jesuit society. The real old-fashioned latch, the only protection and means of opening and closing my front door, responded to the touch of coming and going Fathers from West and North. I had the pleasure of welcoming the first Benedictines on their way to Kansas, and took the liberty of telling them their ultimate home would be Atchison.

Let me tell you, my dear editor, this thing of writing so long and cudgelling my memory is no easy job, besides you know the frost of other days has made the joints of my fingers stiff, almost numb. God bless your paper, the Banner, and God bless you for giving me a chance to live with friends of other days.

Anon,

B. DONNELLY.

CHAPTER XIX.

FATHER DONNELLY, THE MAN.

IN stature Father Donnelly stood about five feet six inches tall. His features were strong and prominent and his complexion in health ruddy. His shoulders were unusually wide and his frame well knitted, showing great physical strength. He was a very counterpart in physical structure of his friend, Father De Smet. It is said of Father De Smet that when a young man in the novitiate near St. Charles the work he did in lifting and carrying on his shoulders trunks and limbs of trees would equal what we read in legendary lore of giants, or what we see done today in circuses and shows by the strong man. But the strong man, the athlete of today, is old and broken at thirty-five years. Father Donnelly, like Father De Smet, did not break or bend under his great feats, and those feats were not at long intervals, but every little while. Father Donnelly would take his share at lifting or moving large slabs of stone, and always insisted that he should be alone on his side of the stone. His awkwardness on horseback as he rode the first time from Kansas City Landing to Independence soon disappeared. He in a short while mastered his horse and many a time offered his services to break in unruly and bucking animals unused to saddle or harness. He often mounted on strong-jawed western horses and would cry out a dare to wager that the beast would not dislodge his tall stove-pipe hat. That hat and Father seemed inseparable. He wore it in all weathers and everywhere except in the Sanctuary and on the church grounds. But even then while preaching he would sometimes have the

hat brought to him and would hold it in his right
hand as he emphasized his remarks or gesticulated.
He was gifted with a wonderful force of character
and aggressive to a remarkable degree.   He had
all his faculties under perfect control.

His daily walks were long and uninterrupted
except to speak to some passerby about the weather
or prospects of the coming greatness of the city
or country.   The man digging in the streets or the
foundations of buildings, or in the field, would
attract him as the magnet does the steel.   He had
to view and suggest how the workman might im-
prove his style or method of handling shovel or
pick.   He would often take the tool from the laborer's hand and give him a demonstration of how
speed and efficiency might result.   A house in
course of erection would make him go out of his
way.   The materials would be carefully examined,
the price of the edifice would be discussed, and
then the history of the original purchase of the
property and the various transfers from the government ownership.   The civil engineer would as-
sert itself in him and he would step off the front
and rear of the property and wind up by telling
the square yards in it, and the cubic feet of the
dislodged earth.   He found his way regularly to
where a hill impeded a projected street and the
next man he met would have to listen to the time
it would take to tear down the hill and what it
would cost to do so, the number of dirt wagons it
would fill and the time required by a.given number
of laborers to do the work.   He was personally
acquainted with every contractor, many of them
had secured their contracts through his influence
with the city officials, and the very men swinging
the picks and shoveling were brought here by him.
As those men were all Catholics and his parishioners he rounded his conversation by advising

them about their religious duties and with em-
phasis would tell them, "My men, your greatest
danger is strong drink and your only chance of
success in life is to keep out of saloons." When
he heard that any of them were indulging too much,
he would urge them to take Father Mathew's pledge
immediately. He would remove his hat, order the
men to uncover and lift their hands and repeat
the words of the temperance pledge. Then he
would take their names and homes or boarding
places, and hasten to tell the employer that the poor
fellows would be straight for the future. Many
a time he would appear at some shop or place where
weak men were laboring, take their week's wage
from them and bring it to their wives and families,
or put it away for them in some secure bank. He
did not wait for Sunday to teach his people industry and saving habits, but did his preaching whenever he met them. He was always moving around
where good might be done. He never tired of
teaching a love for the foreigner's new country;
he was forever extolling the advantages of America "Help your poor friends in dear old Ireland,
induce them to come here, and talk less and dream
less of the old country, and never tire of looking
up the opportunities before you in the broad fields
of America. You were farmers in Ireland, and
keep your eyes on your first trade; put something
by and become farmers. The country life in America is ideal." He sought out opportunities to purchase farms and would tell the cost price, as well
as what was the most productive land. Jackson
County was his first choice, but the new agricultural country over in Kansas was good and very
cheap. He induced a colony of new arrivals here
to purchase a large district near the Missouri River
where they flourished and grew rich. He would
ride over to see them occasionally and encourage

and advise them as to the newest and best methods
of farm production. That colony was ever afterwards thanking him, and in the great procession
which followed his remains to St. Mary's Cemetery they formed a large and conspicuous part,
they swelled the mourning ranks.

Father Donnelly was always loyal to the land
of his forefathers. He loved its scenery, he would
picture its rivers, its many streams of clear water,
its beautiful lakes. Its soil, he ever maintained,
was unequaled the world over. But the blight of
tyranny hung over Ireland. The prospects of a
Free Ireland did not appear promising if at all
possible. He was very matter-of-fact and would
reason that it is better to live untrammeled in
America and keep living than to die trying to free
Ireland. He said on one public occasion that it was
more praiseworthy and more sensible to free Ireland by inducing its people to come in a body to
America than to remain in suffering and in want
fighting against the mighty odds and the infernal
cruelty of the English Government. "Fate," he
would continue, "is as relentlessly cruel to Ireland
as is its brutish oppressor. Don't go to Heaven
as a martyr—come to America, and when you die
go to God as a saint. The fevers and the famines
and the weather as well are all against our Mother-
land." In the '70s and '80s Ireland was visited with
frequent loss of crops, and appeals to America were
met by generous response.

Such sentiments, freely and boldly expressed,
brought forth many criticisms and made many of
his countrymen think of Father Donnelly as one
who did not love his native land. "My native land
was not so kind to me as I am helpful to it," he
would reply. He seems to have sided with the
Young Irelands of 1847. Some of the leaders were
of his time and age. He sent liberally in answer

to the appeals made in America.   He lived to call
the results of the uprising a "fizzle"—not even
worth the money America alone sent to its help
and success.   Before that time and ever after, he
was a great admirer of Daniel O'Connell and his
methods of peaceful protest.   When the Fenians'
fight for the freedom of Ireland was heralded he
turned a deaf ear, and by way of change, sometimes a very bitter tongue against England and the
Fenians.   All new efforts against England for Ireland's good, down to the Parnell Movement, were
looked at askance and with indifference.   He openly
and, in some New York correspondence, in many
letters said unfriendly things against the Fenian
agitators.   "They are," he writes, in the New York
Times, "the most modern.   Their end will be the
usual fight on each other.   Tell the Irish to come
over and go to work and grow up with this country."   He certainly was true to this principle.   No
man, at least west of the Ohio, did so much in
inducing his countrymen to leave home for our
shores.   A firm of Irishmen in St. Louis, the
O'Brien Brothers, kept the Missouri Pacific Railroad growing westward by supplying Irish laborers.
They sent Father Donnelly a New Year's gift in
1857 and wrote to him and had printed in the St.
Louis Republic about the same time, that Father
Donnelly induced more Irishmen to come from Ireland to Missouri than they themselves had.

CHAPTER XX.

HIS LIBRARY.

LONG before Father Donnelly left his native land never to return he was conversant with American history and geography. He had on his person a copy of the Constitution of the United States. He purchased it in Ireland on his first visit to Dublin when he was a young student. It was printed at Boston in the year 1816. He had read it and reread it until he knew it by heart. His reading made him familiar with the lives of Washington and the signers of the Declaration of Independence, also the biographies of American jurists, generals and statesmen. Lincoln, Douglas, Clay, Calhoun, and Benton he greatly admired and could discuss their sayings and repeat passages from their speeches. The history of the various states from the Pilgrim landing to the new state of Kansas was at the tips of his fingers. He put America first among the nations. It was his new, his beloved country. He would on every possible occasion urge his countrymen to love their new country and be true to it.

Father Donnelly carried a greater supply of useful and high-grade knowledge in his later years than in younger days, for he was always adding to his store and trying never to forget by constantly keeping up an acquaintance with everything new in science, history and art. Protoplasms, nebular theories, new and startling ventures in the field of philosophy, spiritism, all that the best magazines of the '60s and '70s and the newest books in literature were sending forth, were conned over, reread and pondered. He believed in security first and as a lever to keep himself properly balanced

he kept at his elbow his dear old St. Thomas, and
Kenrick's, Gury's, and Perrone's theologies.   When
treatise after treatise on ontology fell under the
scrutinizing eye of Rome he would say, "I wish the
Holy Father would cut out all philosophical class-
books in our schools and put in their stead St.
Thomas of Aquin."   His prayer was heard, but his
hearing was closed in death a little while before.
In literature he loved Moore and quoted from him
as he did from Virgil and Horace.   The American
poets were dear to his heart and frequently on his
lips.   Bishop Martin Spalding he believed sur-
passed all the Church writers in America, for his
writings appealed to the people and were educational.   The Boston Pilot was a weekly visitor in
his home and its columns held many a contribution
by him.   But the Catholic editors he rated the highest were Dr. Brownson, McMaster of the Freeman's
Journal and Father Phelan of the Western Watch-
man.   He often found fault with them, but he
would amend his criticisms in a moment by saying,
"They are par excellence the bravest and ablest
defenders of the Church in America."

In the pulpit Father Donnelly excelled as a
plain, thorough expositor of the Gospels.   He evidently prepared himself for his Sunday sermons.
His language was simple and his words were short
and Anglo-Saxon.   He carefully avoided the verbi-
age of the Irish sermon books.   "It's not English
at all, but a turning of words from Latin to English
endings.   Avoid the books of sermons from abroad;
they have long words by men who finished their
English courses in Spain, Rome, Douay, and Lou-
vain.   The adults of your parish do not know the
meaning of these words and the younger genera-
tion will think you are speaking a foreign tongue.
Study, young man, the works of Addison and Steele.
Keep away from the un-English translations from

the French and Spanish done by French and Spanish writers, they will injure your style of expression and fall upon the unwilling and unreceptive ears of the American listeners."

In his spiritual devotions Father Donnelly was regular and frequent. He sought the inside of the railing of the Sanctuary to pray his daily rosary, and he might be found any forenoon at ten o'clock reciting the parts of his office and again at six p. m. It was only when the weather was too cold that he turned from the Sanctuary to the slight comfort of his sitting-room. The church stove was never lighted except on Sundays and holy days of obligation. No church in Kansas City up to Father Donnelly's demise ever had a fire on week days. Steam, hot water, hot air furnaces, were unknown outside of St. Louis, and few of the churches there had the comfort of heat except on Sunday. While in his study and within the church property, and when not in his quarry or brickyard nearby, he might be seen with cassock and beretta, or, as he persistently called it, bonicari—he remembered that name from his seminary days. In ceremonies of the Sanctuary he was most tenacious of his training at the Barrens. His Italian and French professors there were his models in many ways. "Were there no other priests there in your day?" he was asked. "Oh, yes, there were, but they were usually busy on the outside. They figured in the long sick calls and in parish work." The Vincentians' missions went from Perry County, Missouri, down through the vast Territory and State of Texas. This would make him reminiscent, and he would recount the hardships and apostolic zeal of the old professors and priests of the Barrens. He put them on a par with the Jesuits of the West. "But the great and tireless Jesuits died in their Society. The Lazarists were losing their ablest men in the sciences and the most zealous in the missions, by promotion to the mitre. They never sought the honors of the episcopate—they were forced on them by the Holy See. But the Jesuits in the case of De Smet, when he was selected by Rome on one or two occasions for the mitre, worked matters with the Propaganda at Rome to retain him." Bishops Odin, Rosatti, Dominec, Lynch, Ryan, and Timon, strong men, all, were Lazarists. Miege of Leavenworth was a Jesuit. He filled his high position with honor and apostolic zeal, but his home priests were Jesuits, and the Jesuit rule and Jesuit atmosphere permeating his episcopal residence made one imagine he was within a Jesuit community house. In time, after doing his work well, Bishop Miege doffed the mitre and in black cassock and plain beretta lived for years back in the Society of Jesus.

Between his residence near Broadway and westward to what is today Washington Avenue, Father Donnelly cultivated peach, apple and cherry trees. Strawberries and other small fruits grew luxuriantly along the outskirts of the property. When the season had ripened the fruit he shared the luscious products with the Sisters of St. Joseph. Then he would meet the neighbors' children and invite them to come into his garden, and on stated days and hours, and under his eyes, fill themselves. "Take home some to your parents and don't injure the trees by breaking the limbs." How often, in these after years, one may hear lawyers, doctors, and business men tell of the treats Father Donnelly gave them in their boyhood days!

He loved to stop and converse with children, and how fatherly he would place his hand on their heads and bid them be good, and bless their futures. When he daily visited his school rooms it was to encourage the pupils and to arouse their ambition to be good and useful citizens. He was impatient and unwilling to hear from the teachers the pranks and faults of the scholars.   It would cut his visit short if complaints came from the teacher's lips. "That will do, never mind, you were once children and you are good now," he would say, as he hastened down to the door.   Little ones would rush from their homes to get his benevolent smile and good word as he passed along.   He believed candy and cakes were good diet for the children and out of his bulging pockets he distributed to his loved little chums.   Occasionally he went from one school house to another on his morning stroll.   It was never to examine or puzzle the young minds with questions, so he never interfered with the teacher's method or order.   He had been a teacher himself and he had confidence in the teacher and would not injure his standing in his own realm by question or advice.

Two-thirty o'clock every Saturday afternoon and on the days before solemn feasts found him in the confessional where he remained until the supper hour, then back again until the last person left for home; and on Sundays before the Masses he resumed his place as confessor.   He said his two Masses at convenient hours.   On the altar he was graceful and exact in every point of the ritual. His devotion to the sick was marked.   He hurried to the bedside of the patient and his sympathy for the sufferer was that of a father.   He cheered and, when needed, encouraged.   As death approached, his visits were more frequent and his prayers by the bedside of the dying were eloquent of hope and pleading.

Almost from his arrival and while resident pastor of Independence, Father Donnelly saw with the growth of southwest Missouri the certainty of a bishop's see, and that the location of that see would be Kansas City.   Early in 1870 he felt that the time was ripe for at least an agitation for the new diocese. Father Donnelly was not given to letter writing as a habit; in fact, he called "cacoethes scribendi" a mania. But he would and did write letters when there was a need, and one was at hand. At that time the Province of St. Louis embraced Santa Fe, Denver, Omaha, St. Paul, Dubuque, Milwaukee, Chicago, Alton, Green Bay, Leavenworth and Nashville. He began a series of letters to the archbishop and everyone of the suffragans. It was indeed a series, for he wrote at intervals of three months for five years. Before the result was accomplished the whole Province knew that there was a Kansas City and a Southwest Missouri. The various Bishops became quite well acquainted with Father Donnelly's style of chirography and finally yielded to his cogent reasons. The question of a new bishop at Kansas City was acted on favorably at a meeting of the bishops in His Grace's residence in 1879. Three names of deserving priests were sent to Rome. It was said the action was unanimous. Two rather unusual occurences followed the gathering of the bishops. One was that the priests of Milwaukee learned the names on the Terna, and presuming that they had as much right to divulge the choice of the bishops as had the bishop who gave them the information, made it public; the other was that another of the bishops had changed his mind about the need, yes, the justice of placing two bishops in Western Missouri. This bishop visited Kansas City, called on Father Donnelly, and went with him to St. Teresa's Academy to look at a map of Missouri in one of the classrooms. He marked out a large area of the contemplated diocese where there were no Catholics at all. He seemed well acquainted with the population of the little cities and the difficulties of the few priests to maintain themselves.

"Why, St. Joseph is too small territorially, and too meager in point of Catholics, for a diocese. To erect another diocese in this part of Missouri would be an injustice to St. Joseph and would make two bishops suffer almost for want instead of one, as is the case now." He said he was on his way to Rome, and in a few days started. In the course of a year Rome was heard from. The Bishop of St. Joseph was transferred to Kansas City and St. Joseph was made tributary to the city on the Kaw. Father Donnelly lived to hear the decision of Rome. His ambition for Kansas City's recognition was attained.

CHAPTER XXI.

FATHER DONNELLY ATTENDS A BANQUET.

FATHER DONNELLY was not a regular correspondent among his brothers of the ministry. He seldom visited them and they rarely found an excuse to visit the little unkept city on the Kaw. His aloofness gained him the name of being a recluse and lacking in hospitality. In St. Louis where clergymen were weighed and measured for a standing, Father Donnelly was heard of only through the young assistants who had done their bit under his rigorous rules. The picture they painted of him would hardly come up to the colorful and cheerful canvasses of a Leonardo da Vinci! They belonged to the school that preceded the great artists of the golden Florentine days. They depicted him in sombre and unresponsive hues. The daily breakfasts of gruel, the slightly better dinners, the suppers with meat but once a week, and that a boiled chicken, reduced their weight and depressed their spirits. They soon tired of the mountain air which wafted over the sandy plains of Kanzas. Well, their stay with Father Donnelly was usually short, and they petitioned a return to St. Louis and never more of the West if they could help it. They drew for their inquirers a portrait of a man unkept in dress, severe in manner, and critical of youth, who harnessed his curates down to the routine of their clerical duties. Simply that and nothing more. He provided them a comfortable room on a plot of ground six hundred feet or more from the church, where he paid them a morning visit, but let it be known that they were not by Western courtesy expected to return it.

When Westport was a mission tributary to Father Donnelly's parish his assistant was permitted to say Mass there on Sundays and Holydays of obligation. It was "within walking distance." up against a gradual elevation to a high level from which the country around could be viewed. The pastors who had the services of these young men after they had graduated under Father Donnelly said they were tractable to docility. It was by that class of priests that Father Donnelly was made known in St. Louis. From his ordination until his death, a space of thirty-five years, he had visited St. Louis very seldom, possibly four or five times, and then called only on his classmates. Father Donnelly was as little known in St. Louis as a missionary in some distant land. It was said and believed that Father Donnelly was years and years behind the times, almost an antediluvian.

The Tuesday after Bishop P. J. Ryan's consecration, which took place April 14th, 1872, all the visiting archbishops, bishops and attending priests partook of a banquet in his honor given by the priests of the diocese. The banquet was in the beautiful and spacious hall in Pezolt's new restaurant on Olive Street near 10th. The spread was the supreme effort of that far-known caterer. Following the banquet, speeches were made by bishops and archbishops. Bishop Foley, not yet two years in the episcopacy, Bishop of Chicago, and native of Baltimore, made the speech of the day. He was young and handsome, with all the refinement possible, with southern accent, and with a flow of wit and humor that brought forth applause. He was playfully funny in his references to the guest of honor, Bishop Ryan. He spoke of him as a babe two days old. He referred to his swaddling clothes. He exalted Chicago, and mentioned St. Louis as too old for

so young a bridegroom.   He saw archbishop's
honors coming to Chicago, and St. Louis doing the
best it could to survive until finally it would lean
on Chicago as an outside town rests on an adjoining metropolis.   And indeed, St. Louis might yet
be the residing place of the Vicar-General of Chicago!   The printed order of toasts ran out with
Bishop Foley's speech.   Bishop Ryan arose to
thank his friends.   He graciously, and with emo-
tion in eye and accent, thanked all present for
their kindness.   He referred to his happy years
in the priesthood of St. Louis, the many favors received at the hands of his fellow priests, and ten-
derly acknowledged the great dignity to which he
was raised by Archbishop Kenrick, who was ever
to him a Father as well as a Bishop.   He merely
referred to the pleasantries of Bishop Foley.   The
speech was well-prepared and at times delivered
in his best oratorical style.   The occasion evidently
seemed to him too solemn to be marred by banter-
ing.   The St. Louis priests wished and demanded
that some one get back at Bishop Foley.   It was
in order to adjourn, but the priests wanted another speech.   They shouted to Father O'Brien,
the toastmaster, for just one more speech; Father
O'Brien arose and waved silence.   When quiet
came, he said: "Gentlemen, there's something
lacking.   You want one more speech and so do I.
There is a priest here who can make that speech.
You young clergymen don't know, perhaps there
are not more than a dozen of the older ones who
do know, him.   I know him.   We were classmates,
we were ordained side by side.   I now call on
Father Donnelly of Kansas City to arise.   He is
sitting away down near the end of this room."
Father arose and as he walked up to the speakers'
and bishops' table, the priests stood up and
cheered.   There was a smile on his face which

lightened up his countenance. He was attired in a well fitting clerical suit, fresh from the tailor. They saw an intellectual face and a finely shaped head. In a clear, distinct voice and with the greatest possible composure he began. Compliments all around was his introduction. Father Tom Burke, the Lazarist, was kindly referred to, and Father John McGary, also a Lazarist. The latter was the second president of Mount St. Mary's, at Emmetsburg. He was the priest who hired young John Hughes as gardener around the college, and who taught the young man Latin and introduced him into the seminary. Turning to Bishop Foley he congratulated him on his handsome looks and fine speech. His wit as well as his name gave evidence of his race. He was the very man to rule the destinies of the go-ahead Chicago. And if the Bishop may be taken as a revified cinder of the burned city, it would seem as if Chicago was ready for another blaze. Chicago from its infancy had been aglow. When Rome created a diocese in the little village on Lake Michigan, it sent a bishop from the largest city in the land, New York. Full of New York's snap and vigor, Bishop Quarters did superhuman work in a few years, and was satisfied to die. The Vice-Provincial of the Jesuits at St. Louis, a man of zeal, gifted with the shrewdness for which the members of that Society are noted, took up where the New York Bishop let go. In less than three years Bishop Van Der Velde was begging to be allowed to seek a home and work in a quieter realm and was happy to be awarded the see of Natchez, Mississippi. He breathed easier in his sunny southern home. The third apostle, with the fight of St. Paul in his heart and the books of a professor of philosophy and theology in his head, and with the constitution of an athletic and a heavy Irish brogue born with him in Connaught and

growing with his growth, left the seminary in St.
Louis, determined to conquer or die, but never to
resign. His first day in Chicago loosened up something vital inside of him. Five years in the breezes
of Lake Michigan made him feel a longing for a
little rest in the balmy atmosphere of Italy. Distance did not lend enchantment to the view, and
he took up his home in the soothing fogs of London to act as bishop auxiliary to Cardinal Archbishop Wiseman. Then the polished, gentle
Bishop Duggan left behind his coadjutorship in St.
Louis and went forward to propitiate the elements
in Chicago. He still lives, in the confinement of
St. Vincent's Hospital, in this city. Baltimore,
steeped in southern culture, quiet in the repose of
peace and brotherly contentment, offers its most
beloved priest, secretary to a Kenrick and a Spalding, as a pacificator in heart and mind and tongue,
eloquent and suave, to make a long reign. You
came, you saw, and no doubt you'll conquer. Your
aspirations are high and noble. You predict great
growth and pleasant results. You have thrown out
your line of diocesan advancement. You predict
the future great Chicago will cross the Mississippi
and you plant a Vicar-General in St. Louis, where
an archbishop now reigns. In your short and
happy term in Chicago you have outstepped even
your city's aspirations. But there is a far-looking
strength and greatness in the Church ruler of St.
Louis, and there is a wit and cunning in the babe
of two days who now peeps out of his swaddling
clothes. Chicago is not a salubrious climate for
bishops, and it would be well to keep the Vicar
General nearer the Lake than St. Louis. Bishops
need their vicars close at home. They are helpful
stays near the diocesan throne."

He said many more things, and when he returned to his place among the younger clergy,

plaudits were ringing through the festal chamber.
Priests were rushing from their seats to shake his
hand and thank him.   His former assistants came
forward to convince themselves it was the Father
Donnelly they had served for short spaces in suc-
cession in Kansas City.

St. Joseph's Orphan Asylum

CHAPTER XXII.

LAST DAYS.

ON the feast of the Annunciation, 1880, Fathers Dunn and Kiely, and two Redemptorists, Fathers Faivre and Firley, were guests of the pastor of that church. Father Donnelly preached at the solemn high Mass. After dinner Father Donnelly surprised the priests when he told them he had written his resignation. He read them the letter to Archbishop Kenrick. His brother priests reasoned long and well with him to reconsider, but it was no use. He said his health required rest and quiet. In a few days the resignation was forwarded. During Holy Week a letter from His Grace came to Father Donnelly. It read as follows:

"Rev. Dear Father Donnelly: Father Doherty, pastor of Kirkwood, will take charge of Immaculate Conception Church on the coming Easter Sunday.
Yours truly,
†P. R. KENRICK, Abp."

Short and to the point. No time was lost in the writing of that letter. There was no time for a recognition of his thirty-five years of apostolic work, no time to say a word of thanks for the financial wealth he had so freely given Independence, Westport, and Kansas City, and the St. Louis Arch-diocese. A few weeks previously Father Donnelly wrote three letters detailing some of the gifts of property he gave the Church at those places, and the cash he had expended out of his own personal means. He stated in those letters that he was nearing his end from disease, and also wrote that he was now without a cent of money or a foot of real estate. The same information ran through each of the letters, a copy of which follows:

"Parsonage, Kansas City, Jan. 19, 1880.

"I am sure you will be pleased to hear that an Orphan Asylum is now completed and paid for; the entire cost is $16,000. The sum of $11,200 was obtained for this purpose from the sale of a part of the original ten-acre lot left by Father Le Roux, which I saved for a period of thirty-five years; the balance I saved out of our new Catholic Cemetery, with every dollar I could spare for three years. I also donated ten acres of land situated near the Redemptorist Convent, which I bought sixteen years ago for a cemetery. There is no debt on the new cemetery. Its 44 acres I purchased with my own money. I purchased the site of the Westport Church and reduced the debt on the new church started by Father Doherty.

"Now I do not own a square foot of real estate on the face of the earth, or a dollar in money. Some future pastor or perhaps a bishop will probably build a cathedral here and bring the people and the needs of religion to greater perfection. As for me, my course is nearly run. I suffer from chest disease. I have never had a vacation.

"Kansas City is surely to become one of the large cities of the United States. Buildings are going up all the winter, the present year is expected to be the most prosperous of all. The population at present is estimated at 60,000. The writer is as much astonished at what he sees, although it so happened that he was around here before the city was founded at all, as those who have come lately.

"Affectionately yours,
"BERNARD DONNELLY"

Three copies of this letter were written, one to Archbishop Kenrick, another to Bishop Ryan, coadjutor bishop, and a third to Father Muehlsiepen, V. G. of St. Louis.

Father Doherty, the successor, arrived here on the Saturday before Easter Sunday. Father Donnelly's greeting to him was cordial. He said, "This is your parish, and this is the only home I have to give you." Taking his hat and overcoat he moved to the door, saying, "God bless you; may your days here be long and happy." Father Doherty replied to Father Donnelly: "I want you to stay, this will be your home as long as you live. I'll find quarters somewhere in the parish until the people build me a residence." It was no use. Father Donnelly went forth. He had no home in sight, he had no money to purchase food or shelter. As he moved outside to the streets, some Sisters from St. Joseph's Hospital passing by hailed him and hearing his story, said to him· "Father Donnelly, the Sisters of St. Joseph owe you all they have in Kansas City. They foresaw what was coming and there is a comfortable room awaiting you in St. Joseph's Hospital." They retraced their steps to the hospital and bade Father Donnelly go with them, where he would have a home and care as long as he lived.

His remaining days were not many. Disease was weakening him. When the sun shone he would move around. His steps were slow and tottering, but the smile of recognition as he met a friend here and there lit his wan face. In November he went to bed to get up no more. The attention of the good Sisters was unremitting. All that physicians could do was exhausted, and a few minutes past 4 p. m., December 15th, 1880, Father Donnelly's soul went back to his God, who does not forget and who repays for services rendered. It was a coincidence, it was by the direction of a moving Spirit, it was a coming together that was not arranged for—every priest in Kansas City, without a call from anybody, without a knowledge of his coming dissolution, was at Father Donnelly's bedside when his spirit went forth. The day previous and the morning of the day of his death, the inquiring clergy were told that Father Donnelly had rested the night before and would likely survive several days. The writer, who knew him longest and best, was the first to reach his side. Death was coming very fast. Before he had read far in the prayers for the dying, the priests were all kneeling in the sick chamber and answering the invocations for a happy death. The Sisters, too, were there from the parish schools, from St. Teresa's Academy, and the Sisters of the hospital. When the end had come, priests and Sisters lingered to pray for the departed. A worthy man, a true priest, and an indefatigable worker had left the scene of years of truly apostolic zeal for the glory of God and the good of man.

Early in the afternoon before the day of the funeral, the children of the Immaculate Conception Parish, and of Annunciation and St. Patrick's, followed by fully two thousand people from all parts of the city, escorted Father Donnelly's remains to his church. When the procession arrived at Broadway and 11th Streets there was a crowd awaiting the corpse, that filled sidewalks and streets up to the church doors. The aisles and pews were packed to the Sanctuary. It was one dense throng of mourning friends and admirers, who showed by their tears and sobs that a loved Father was dead. All during the night there was a stream of people passing in and out after viewing the remains. Volunteers gave their services to leading in the rosary and litanies that never died out for a moment until the first tones of the organ announced the hour for the Requiem services and the entrance into the Sanctuary of over one hundred priests from St. Louis and all the cities and towns in the West. One hundred priests forty years ago meant more than lived east and west of the banks of the Missouri River this side of St. Louis. The solemn High Mass was chanted and every priest present went with the funeral cortege out to the new Mount St. Mary's Cemetery to see the remains of a great priest buried within the cemetery he donated and in the grave he selected, where he often said he wished to sleep for all time—but, without rest in life, his tired bones were not to be allowed to rest in death.

The irony of fate seemed to follow' Father Donnelly into the grave. Sunday after Sunday he declaimed against the extravagant funeral processions that conveyed the dead to the cemeteries. "You, my dear people," he would say, "go to extremes in your lavish expenditures at funerals. You spend money you cannot afford on carriages and buggies; you incur debts and are forced to deny yourselves and your families becoming attire and the necessities of life as a result. At times many of you have lost your jobs by staying away from your places of employment a half and frequently a whole day in going and coming from the cemetery. When death enters your homes you spend so recklessly you are indebted to undertaker and carriage owners for months."

When the news of Father Donnelly's death was spread abroad numbers of his friends met in a public hall to arrange for a funeral that would show their appreciation of a good priest and citizen. A committee was appointed. A brass band was first on their list, then carriages for pallbearers and for friends unable to bear the expense of conveyances for themselves. They selected a coffin costing over $900. Such a display has never been equalled in the history of Kansas City, even to the present day. The newspapers the following day said there were 118 buggies, 75 carriages, 3 omnibusses, and 22 other vehicles, making in all 219 conveyances in the procession, which was two miles long and required forty-five minutes to pass a given point.

Father Donnelly had often concluded his remonstrances against the extravagance and show of modern funerals with the remarks, "When I am dead I shall not have need of a will, for I shall have no money to distribute. I want a plain pine-board coffin, and wish no display of carriages and buggies."

When the undertaker had drawn up his statement of the costs, he could find no person or persons willing to assume any financial responsibility —they had acted as a committee only. All of Father Donnelly's own property had been given to the churches and educational and charitable institutions during his lifetime. A deed returned to Father Donnelly by Archbishop Kenrick about the time of his death, and found several weeks after his burial, furnished the means of a final settlement of his funeral expenses.

Father Donnelly's remains rested for a time in Mount St. Mary's Cemetery, his personal gift to the Catholics of Kansas City. When the new Cathedral was completed they were taken from the grave and placed beneath a side aisle in the Sanctuary. He lies in the original ten acres left by Father Le Roux and so carefully guarded by him against the efforts of committees to sell it or exchange it, or to partition it for the erection of new parishes.

Peace to your soul, Kansas City's great Pastor and Provider! Your sagacity did more to build the Cathedral than did the contributions of Kansas City's Catholics. Your loving care provided an asylum for the orphan, a hospital for the sick and the dying, and a cemetery for the dead. You opened the first school for the little ones of your flock, and out of your savings helped erect the first academy for higher education. Your loyalty to your city in counsel and assistance when it was a struggling landing-place was side by side with your efforts in upbuilding the cause of religion. Your zeal for Kansas City and for its growth to your oft-predicted metropolitan greatness had no selfish motive. Your grave has no marker of silver or brass to tell where your ashes lie. No shaft of marble points heavenward in cemetery, park or boulevard to say that you were Kansas City's faithful friend and helper in its infancy and in its struggling days when war and nature's obstacles threatened its very life. But your memory is kept alive by the property you donated to and preserved for the Church, by the institutions of charity and learning you were instrumental in founding, by the presence of those religious orders (both men and women) who came at your invitation—yes, verily by your works, oh good and faithful servant in the vineyard of the King of kings, are you known and remembered in the place where you accomplished so much good. ETERNAL REST IN HEAVEN, Father Donnelly, is the prayer of the writer of your long-deferred Biography and will stand as

F I N I S

Note

ACKNOWLEDGMENT is hereby gratefully made for the photographs so kindly furnished the author;

To D. P. Thomson
    for the portrait of Father Donnelly.

To The Photographic and View Company
    for the pictures of Father Donnelly's Church
    St. Joseph's Orphan Asylum, and the two views
    of St. Teresa's Academy.

To Anderson Photo Company
    for the views of Redemptorist Church.

CPSIA information can be obtained at www.ICGtesting.com
Printed in the USA
LVOW06s0309080815

449370LV00012B/319/P